The Way of
Wicca
A Practical Guide to Your Spiritual Awakening

responsibility of the recipient reader. Under no circumstances will any legal responsibility or blame be held against the publisher for any reparation, damages, or monetary loss due to the information herein, either directly or indirectly.

Respective authors own all copyrights not held by the publisher.

The information herein is offered for informational purposes solely and is universal as so. The presentation of the information is without contract or any type of guarantee assurance.

The trademarks that are used are without any consent, and the publication of the trademark is without permission or backing by the trademark owner. All trademarks and brands within this book are for clarifying purposes only and are the owned by the owners themselves, not affiliated with this document.

Table of Contents

Introduction

Mention Wicca, paganism or witchcraft, and there will be people who believe the three terms are synonymous and interchangeable, but that is not how it actually works. The etymology of the term Wicca means 'to bend,' or 'to shape.' That's appropriate, because Wicca as a religion is indeed flexible, and can be shaped to suit the beliefs and requirements of each individual practitioner.

Many Wiccan rituals and practices are based on the centuries-old traditions and beliefs of witchcraft, yet it is, above all things, a modern religion. And make no mistake, Wicca is more about religion and spiritual practice than magic and casting spells. That said, some practitioners are more involved with the magical and herbal aspects of Wicca. In this book, though, we will be concentrating on how Wicca works as a modern religion, in a time when people are moving away from established, formal religions to find their own spiritual paths as world events are becoming more and more difficult to make sense of.

This book will examine in detail what it means to be a Wiccan practitioner in the 21st century, now that Wicca and other alternative spiritual practices and religions are no longer hidden in the shadows. These days, Wiccans can be more open about their practices than ever before, although many still prefer to work in the background, anonymously, rather than be too open about their beliefs.

Modern Wicca was developed early in the 20th century and unveiled as a new religion in 1954 by Gerald Gardner, a retired British Civil Servant. The final repeal of the last of the laws against witchcraft in 1951 meant that Gardner, and many other witches and Wiccans, were at last able to practice their craft openly, rather than keeping their beliefs under wraps.

Gardner's two books – *Witchcraft Today* and *The Meaning of Witchcraft* –served to renew interest in witchcraft or the Old Religion. His version of Wicca also incorporated elements of diverse religions, including the tenets of Kabbalah. These days, there are a number of different Wiccan traditions, including Alexandrian, British Traditional Wicca, Eclectic and Gardnerian, which is, of course, named after Wicca's founding father.

Wiccans worship The Triple Goddess of the Moon, in her distinct and very different stages of Maiden, Mother, and Crone, as well as the

Horned God of the Wilds. In common with other religions, they also believe in reincarnation and a version of karmic payback. Wiccans practice spiritual magic, and they are very much in tune with Nature and ecology. Today, when climate change, renewable energy, and safe waste disposal are universally debated upon, this places them firmly in the mainstream of activists for a better Earth. This means more and more people are identifying with Wiccan ways.

The kingpin of Wiccan practice is based around the Wheel of the Year. This aligns the compass points of North, South, East, and West with the elements of Earth, Air, Water, Fire, and Spirit. Wiccans see the spark of divinity in the Moon and indeed all of Nature, which is at one with the deities, along with every living thing on Mother Earth. In this respect, Wicca can be compared with both witchcraft and paganism, although there are also many disparities between the three belief systems.

As mentioned earlier, in this book, we will introduce and explain the more common beliefs, rituals, and spells that are typically associated with the religion of Wicca. This will be accomplished in a manner that beginners will be able to understand. By the time you finish reading this book, you will be equipped with the knowledge you need to begin to practice Wicca, either as a solo practitioner or as a member of a coven.

The emphasis is on the spiritual side of Wicca rather than the magical aspects, but since magic, spell casting and holistic treatment forms a sizeable element of Wiccan practice, we will touch on these matters as appropriate. There will also be information on starting your own Book of Shadows, the sabbats and esbats of the Wheel of the Year, crystal and energy healing, and all the other things that make Wicca so enjoyable and fulfilling for so many people. Enjoy, and blessed be, children of the Universe!

Chapter 1: What is Wicca, Exactly?

Wicca is, above all things, a very democratic religion, centering on the individual practitioner's personal spiritual path and their attunement with Nature. It's not a cult, and there are no specific leaders or recognized sacred texts. Wiccans read what they believe will further their knowledge and hone their craft, rather than reading the same things as every other Wiccan.

Like Buddhists, Wiccans believe the Divine is present in all living things, and that all living things have souls. It works closely with the Elements of life – Earth, Air, Water, and Fire, along with a fifth element, Spirit. These five Elements are also acknowledged in witchcraft and spiritualism and are physically represented in the five-pointed pentagram. This can be seen on the altars of both Wiccans and witches and is often worn as a pendant by practitioners.

In Wicca, sin, judgment, and punishment are alien concepts, as the belief is that each individual is responsible and accountable for their own actions, and as long as they harm nobody, pretty much anything goes. It follows, then, that there is no Wiccan Heaven or Hell, as acknowledged by various other religions.

Wiccans believe in reincarnation and consider that souls reincarnate to learn essential life lessons they failed to master in previous lifetimes. Alternatively, it may be part of their soul mission to return to help someone else grasp their own life lesson at some point in the future. This doctrine is very closely aligned with the Eastern concept of karma, karmic debt, and karmic payback.

The Wiccan code of morality is designed to help every Wiccan to become the best possible version of themselves. Practitioners work towards their goals by living a good life in this incarnation, helping others, and safeguarding and protecting the Earth and its resources for the benefit of future generations.

Each Wiccan practitioner is encouraged to evaluate their own actions critically, and take responsibility for their words and deeds, both good and bad. There is nothing of the modern blame culture or victim culture in Wicca, which is a refreshing and welcome change at a time when accountability is seemingly out of fashion.

Wiccans – who are essentially white witches – are just ordinary people, wanting to live a good life and help those around them to do the same. Real Wiccan magic doesn't come from a magic wand or a book of spells. It lies in the personal transformation, which often takes place when people wholeheartedly embrace the main teachings of Wicca, thereby improving life for themselves and others, as they work with love and joy in their hearts.

Gerald Gardner and Wicca

As already noted, Wicca has many of its roots in ancient times, and indeed shares a number of characteristics with both paganism and witchcraft. As a distinct, named religion, though, it is a relatively modern invention. Wicca, as we know it today, was articulated early in the 20th century, and was the brainchild of retired British Civil Servant Gerald Gardner.

As well as the two books which rekindled interest in witchcraft after centuries of persecution which meant the craft had to be practiced in secret, Gardner also wrote what he claimed was the first authentic *Book of Shadows*. Although there are no defined sacred texts in Wicca, the Wiccan Rede and the *Book of*

Shadows are each, in their own different ways, cornerstones of Wiccan spiritual practice.

Gardner's version of the *Book of Shadows* was very different from the modern, individual volumes that Wiccans work with and from. It was a teaching tool for his students and members of his coven, rather than a personal record of a practicing Wiccan's spiritual growth and accumulation of knowledge and experience. New initiates to Gardner's coven made their own, handwritten copies of the *Book of Shadows*, to which they later added more personalized entries as they progressed along their Wiccan journey.

The Gardnerian tradition of Wicca is rather like a secret society. New initiates are obliged to take oaths of secrecy on joining. It's pretty much impossible to gain admission into a Gardnerian coven - assuming you can find one in the first place, that is. Ritual nudity is a requirement at meetings, and this tradition is the least flexible of all, following a strictly prescribed spiritual path. Gardnerian Wiccans belong to hierarchical covens, and they must agree to undertake a great deal of study, so it can be very exacting being a Wiccan of the Gardnerian tradition.

Over the years, more information and literature has been published about Gardnerian Wicca than any other Wiccan tradition. Paradoxically though, this branch of the religion remains largely shrouded in mystery to the majority of Wiccans.

Gardner's contemporaries agreed that he was a very funny and charming man, but he could be economical with the truth if it suited his purpose. He died from a heart attack in 1964, aged 79, when he was traveling home to the UK from Lebanon on a Scottish merchant ship. He was buried in Tunis, with just the captain attending.

Fifty years later, on 13 June 2014, Gardner was honored with a blue heritage plaque on the Dorset home he lived in during the 1930s. Eerily, this was unveiled exactly 130 years after he was born. It was also Friday 13, and a full moon! Wiccans and witches set great store by synchronicities, and there are several at work here.

Wicca is a uniquely British religion, with a wide support base in North America and Europe, spreading to other English-speaking countries in the 1960s and 1970s. It's difficult to estimate how many Wiccans there are worldwide, due to the reluctance of practitioners to out themselves, but there could be 3 million or more around the world. It's quite a legacy for Gerald Gardner to leave behind him, isn't it?

The Wiccan Rede

Being a practical and versatile religion, Wicca is mainly concerned with learning and experience rather than theory and theology. Divinity is present within every living thing and is not the exclusive preserve of deities. It's a religion of evolution, which adapts and transforms with each passing generation.

There is no recognized doctrine or even any official Wicca prayers, and there are certainly no 'must-read' textbooks. This means that Wicca is a religion that is truly personal to each individual practitioner. Probably the only text that comes anywhere near a formal statement of Wiccan doctrine is the Rede. It's quite short, so I will reproduce it in its entirety for your reference.

Bide the Wiccan Laws we must In Perfect Love and Perfect Trust.

Live and let live. Fairly take and fairly give.

Cast the Circle thrice about to keep the evil spirits out.

To bind the spell every time let the spell be spake in rhyme.

Soft of eye and light of touch, Speak little, listen much.

Deosil go by the waxing moon, chanting out the Witches' Rune.

Widdershins go by the waning moon, chanting out the baneful rune.

When the Lady's moon is new, kiss the hand to her, times two.

When the moon rides at her peak, then your heart's desire seek.

Heed the North wind's mighty gale, lock the door and drop the sail.

When the wind comes from the South, love will kiss thee on the mouth.

When the wind blows from the West, departed souls will have no rest.

When the wind blows from the East, expect the new and set the feast.

Nine woods in the cauldron go, burn them fast and burn them slow.

Elder be the Lady's tree, burn it not or cursed you'll be.

When the Wheel begins to turn, let the Beltane fires burn.

When the Wheel has turned to Yule, light the log and the Horned One rules.

Heed ye flower, Bush and Tree, by the Lady, blessed be.

Where the rippling waters go, cast a stone and truth you'll know.

When ye have a true need, hearken not to others' greed.

With a fool, no season spend, lest ye be counted as his friend.

Merry meet and merry part, bright the cheeks and warm the heart.

Mind the Threefold Law you should, three times bad and three times good.

When misfortune is enow, wear the blue star on thy brow.

True in love ever be, lest thy lover's false to thee.

Eight words the Wiccan Rede fulfill: An ye harm none, do what ye will.

The first two lines and last two lines encapsulate the abiding spirit of modern Wiccan practice – love, trust, live and let live, and do what you want, as long as it harms nobody. That means you too. Wicca, white witchcraft and spiritualism all operate with love as the foundation for all they do, and before you are able to do good works for others, you must first love and respect yourself. Hopefully, you can relate to that, because it really is important.

The Wiccan Rede may be short and to the point, but in essence, it can be condensed even further to just two short words, and they should be eternally engraved on your soul: 'Harm None.'

How Wicca Differs From Witchcraft

We have already learned that there are a number of similarities between Wicca and Witchcraft, but there are also a lot of differences as well, so those who speak of the two religions interchangeably are mistaken in their understanding.

Wicca is a contemporary version of Paganism. It is a formal religion that has its origins in the veneration of nature. Key themes associated with Wicca include the worship of the God and the Goddess, a belief in the concept of reincarnation, and the use of magic and protective magical circles within prescribed ceremonial rites. That said, Wiccans do not normally use magic as much as practitioners of witchcraft. However, since it is essentially a very individual-centered religion, this may not always be the case.

At the heart of Wiccan practice are the various sabbats, esbats, solstices, equinoxes and other festivals and celebrations tied in with Nature. This comes together in the essentially Wiccan concept of the Wheel of the Year, which we will examine in more detail later in the book. Witches also work with the Wheel of the Year but may not celebrate all the festivals. Wiccans go for the full house, so to speak.

Witchcraft is a blanket term applied to the customs and practices of a witch, who is defined as someone who practices folk magic and has a good working knowledge of herbs. Some Wiccans may call themselves witches, but witches will never call themselves Wiccans if they are purely practitioners of witchcraft.

The term witch is not connected in any way with Satanism, Christianity, or indeed any other religion or belief system. Some Wiccans may also identify as Christians, but witches insist they have nothing to do with Christianity, and their belief system is based on science and nature, rather than religious dogma.

Essentially, witchcraft is about spells, potions, charms, and rituals. Anything a witch may do for themselves or for others can be counted as witchcraft. Again, there is no connection with Satanism or Christianity, although witchcraft is recognized as a religion, and is often referred to, even now, as 'The Old Religion.' It's worth pointing out here that both Wicca and witchcraft are only ever practiced for altruistic purposes – never for evil, to go against Nature or to bend the will of another to your own benefit with the use of power or fear. This is termed black magic, and it bears no relation whatsoever to Wicca or witchcraft.

While practitioners of witchcraft do respect Nature, like Wiccans, they do not worship either Nature or the God and Goddess, and they are more likely to contact the world of Spirit.

Witch magic is generally practical, while Wiccan magic tends to be more slanted towards 'the magic of the mind,' where miracles are created in life by the power of our thoughts and deeds. Both Wiccans and witches subscribe to the tenet of 'The Power of Three,' where what we put out to the Universe is returned to us threefold. So, if you live a good life and are kind to others as a matter of routine, your blessed behavior will return with interest, to create miracles in your life, and that is the Magic of the Mind.

Witches do not observe the 'Harm None' exhortation of the Wiccan Rede, although they do practice good magic, and also believe in respect, honesty, and accountability. However, witches feel justified in using a hex or curse as protection or in self-defense, where a Wiccan is most unlikely to resort to that form of protection.

I could spend a lot of time listing differences and similarities between Wicca and witchcraft, but that would go against the main focus of this book, which is to shed light on the ways of Wicca. So, now you have a pretty good idea of what Wicca is and is not, let's move forward. In Chapter 2, we'll discuss the theoretical aspects of Wicca, and examine the role of energy, the deities and the concept of divinity, animism, the

Hermetic Principles, and the different traditions of Wicca. Blessed Be!

Chapter 2: The Theory of Wicca

As we have already learned, Wicca is a relatively modern religion, developed in the first half of the 20th century by Gerald Gardner, and unveiled following the repeal of the last Witchcraft Laws in the early 1950s. It draws on elements of ancient and modern religions, philosophies and belief systems, as well as reverence for Nature and the doctrine of animism, worship of the Goddess and the God, and the Hermetic Principles. Science and Christianity also have some bearing on Wiccan beliefs and practices.

Satan, Christianity, and Wicca

Before we get into discussing what Wicca is all about, let's clear up once and for all that it is most definitely NOT about. One of the big misconceptions about Wicca and witchcraft, which dates from the time of the persecution of witches in medieval times, is that those who practice witchcraft automatically work with Satan and summon demons.

It's a nasty, undeserved slander – especially since Satan is a Christian concept, while the origins of Wicca date back to pagan, pre-Christian times. During the witch hunts, people would denounce the village wise women as witches if they took a dislike to them and would often state that they had seen her summon Satan to destroy crops or bring other disasters down on the locals. This 'evidence' was taken at face value by fundamentalists who believed that any religion rather than the one they followed was heretical, so you can see how witches ended up with such a bad press!

In Wicca, because of the Wiccan Rede tenet 'Harm None,' nothing is ever defined as sinful, as practicing Wiccans pride themselves on their integrity and love for their companions in the Universe. Since Satan exists as a deterrent and/or punishment in the Christian doctrine, then Wiccans are not devil worshippers, although some Christians have been discovered to be Satanists through the centuries.

Because of ongoing depictions in art since the Middle Ages, the Wiccan Horned God – the symbol of the land, fertility, and power – is compared to Satan because of his wild appearance, with horns, a beard, and often a large phallus. And as 'sacrifices' are made to him, this reinforces the Satan myth. However, Wiccan sacrifice does not involve blood as this would go against the 'Harm None' decree. Offerings to the Goddess and the God are typically food and wine, which is buried or poured into the soil to enrich the Earth and continue the cycle of life.

Wicca and black magic are two completely different philosophies, and while black magic practitioners may summon demons, and even Satan himself, Wiccans work only with benevolent spirits and deities to perform white magic and bring about beneficial changes for people and for the environment, whereas black magic is based on establishing malevolent power over others through fear.

Wicca, Animism, and Nature

Wiccans believe there is an element of the Divine in all of us, and we are all part of The One and all that is. Therefore, the concept of animism – the personification of plants, animals, and other objects finds a logical place in the Wiccan belief system.

Animists believe that everything has a soul and spirit, not just humans, so we shouldn't harm any creature or object at all, since we may cause them unwarranted distress. To animists, everything is spirit rather than matter, so every action, whether to another living thing or inanimate object, has a potential for reaction.

Wiccans may not go along with all animist beliefs, but since they work with crystals and ceremonial objects, which are charged with energy, it's clear, they identify with some aspects of animism. The way Wiccans process animism is with the idea that because so many elements of Nature have souls, then it's up to them, as guardians of the Earth and Nature, to ensure that the spirits of the natural world inhabiting the trees, lakes, and rocks are not offended by the way they are treated. Therefore, offerings to the Earth and the trees, for example, often form an intrinsic element of the Wiccan ritual.

Nature is a great place for releasing negative energies since a walk in the woods or along a seashore can have a wonderful calming effect. The besom – synonymous with witches – is a natural product, made from hawthorn wood, birch twigs, and strips of willow. Its main use is to sweep away negative energy ritually, so it's another example of how Wiccans and witches work in harmony with Nature. Most of the required components for spells come from natural sources too, as do the ingredients of herbal remedies.

Nature also works in close partnership with us – if we plant crops, we are rewarded with food, but if we pollute waters, the consequences can be catastrophic for everyone. Wiccans are very careful to treat all aspects of Nature with due deference and respect and are often ecological activists as well as practicing witches.

The Goddess and the God

Wiccans cheerfully admit that how they worship their deities can be rather complicated for newcomers to the religion to process and understand. They consider The Goddess and The God to be two distinct and equal forces of energy, each forming part of a whole, and each endowed with both male and female characteristics. They are at one with Nature, forming part of the integral whole, rather than assuming omnipotence over it, like the Christian God of creation.

These deities may be referred to by a number of different names or none at all, depending on the customs of different traditions of Wicca. Essentially, though, the God is usually referred to as the Horned God of the Woods. His most appropriate equivalent from ancient mythology is Pan, the Greek god of shepherds, mountains, the forests, and hunting. The God may also be known as Cernunnos, and he is associated with the sun and the Underworld.

God is, like Pan, connected with fertility and lust. In his aspect of the Green Man, he is responsible for the trees and vegetation, and due to his connection with the Underworld, he is said to sing to the souls of the dying, so they pass to spirit without fear.

The Goddess is most frequently known as the Triple Goddess of the Moon, and she is identified with Diana, the Roman goddess of the hunt, who is also strongly connected to the moon. Her three aspects are identified as Maiden, Mother, and Crone, and they correspond to the waxing, full and waning moons of the lunar cycles. Both Pan and Diana also share strong links with Nature and the creatures of the forest.

The God rules the wintertime, the season when in, ancient times, food could only be gathered by hunting. The Triple Goddess, who is also associated with the Earth, rules the summer months.

The founder of Wicca as we know it today - Gerald Gardner – was comfortable with the idea of duo theism, or the worship of two gods. There is evidence that the ancient Britons also worshipped horned gods and mother goddesses. The Wicca God and Goddess, therefore, may, or may not, be derived from the pagan pantheon.

Wicca is a flexible religion, and its practitioners can worship any deities they want to, from any religion or pantheon, not just precursors to Wiccan tradition. Many Wiccans consider naming deities or identifying them as masculine and feminine is irrelevant to their pattern of worship anyway, since all are part of The One, and identifying individual elements just complicates matters further.

Newcomers to Wicca will probably find it simpler, to begin with, the concept of worshipping and making offerings to the identified Triple Goddess and Horned God. Further reading and study may result in a calling to other, more specific deities. Wicca is as flexible as any religion possibly can be, so allow your personal spiritual experience to guide you along your path.

The 7 Hermetic Principles

The 7 Hermetic Principles are universal laws going back to the era of Ancient Rome and Ancient Greece. 'Hermetic' is translated as 'esoteric' or 'occult,' meaning the Hermetic Principles were based on secret knowledge of the Universe, which could only be understood and applied by a select few.

They have been assembled anonymously in the *Kybalion* – an ancient book based on the teachings of the sage Hermes Trismegistus, whose surname means 'three times great.' He was known to have great mastery over all things connected with the three planes of existence in his philosophy – physical, mental, and spiritual. He was known as Thoth in ancient Egyptian culture, and Hermes by the Greeks. Thoth was the Egyptian god of knowledge, magic, and wisdom, while Hermes had superhuman strength and stamina, and was the immortal messenger of the Greek gods.

If you're just switching off and glazing over because you think none of this can possibly be relevant today, maybe you need to reconsider. The secret of the Hermetic Principles is that they must be read as if they were only written recently. In other words, read and digest this information from a 21st-century perspective; otherwise, you will gain very little from it. Let's take a look at each of the principles in detail and examine how they can be applied in Wicca and in our daily lives.

The Principle of Mentalism

This theory predates the scientifically proven evidence that everything is energy, but goes a little further with it, and states 'All is Mind.' In other words, our thoughts influence our actions, so we recreate our own reality, whether we realize it or not. This also dovetails with the Universal Law of Attraction and the Threefold Law.

The lesson here is, be careful what you wish for because you can create your own reality. As powerful, intelligent beings, we have to be sure that what we are creating is what we truly want and consider the implications of our actions on others.

The Principle of Correspondence

The guiding influence of this principle will be very familiar to anyone who works with Spirit; 'as above, so below, as within, so without, as the Universe, so the soul.' Basically, this reinforces what we've already read about. We may think that something we do can hardly affect anyone but those closest to us, but we would be very wrong.

Because we are all connected in some way, then our thoughts or actions can have repercussions on a scale we may not imagine. Also, we create our own reality, so what claims our thoughts most is what our lives will become in the near future. It follows, then, that we must always be aware of our thoughts, and steer away from negativity before it has a chance to entrench itself in our consciousness and becomes our new normal.

The Principle of Vibration

If all is energy – and science has established that this is indeed so – then all is also vibration, because energy is never static. It cannot be contained. Even something like the laptop I am working on now is in a state of vibration, although because it is a dense vibration, I cannot see or feel its movement. One of my favorite spiritual books is *Raise Your Vibration,* by Kyle Gray. In it, he explains that while we cannot change what happens around us, we can change the way we react to events and the way we process them.

If we are in a state of fear, then we are vibrating at a low frequency, but if we can respond in a state of calm acceptance, we raise our vibration, bringing ourselves more into alignment with the vibrations of the Universe. Since we are all connected and all part of The One, then raising our vibrations not only benefits ourselves and the people close to us, it makes a deposit in the Positivity Bank of the Universe, so we are helping many more people than we could ever conceive of.

The Principle of Polarity

'All is dual; all have poles.' You may have heard of the saying 'opposites attract,' but polarity, in this case, is all about degree and balance. Think of the shower you had this morning. You were able to balance the temperature between hot and cold, so you could have a comfortable shower, but what if you could only have a hot or a cold shower? That wouldn't be so comfortable, and life is like that.

It's all a matter of degree. If you always shower in cold water, you'll cause your blood vessels to constrict, and your heart will have to work harder to circulate the blood around your body, so there's a potentially serious health threat here. It will also take longer to warm your body to a comfortable temperature, and it can interfere with the efficiency of your immune system, leaving you vulnerable to infection and disease.

On the other hand, if you always shower in hot water, there are pitfalls in that too. Hot water can dry out your skin, making it uncomfortable, itchy, and even unsightly. If you have an existing skin condition such as acne or eczema, hot showers can make the symptoms even worse, and showering under hot water can increase your blood pressure to dangerous.

It's so much better if you balance the water, so it's just right for you, and life is just like that. Balance fear with confidence, hate with love, and negativity with positivity, both internally and when interacting with others. This will raise your vibrations and benefit everyone.

The Principle of Rhythm

'All is flow, the pendulum swings, and all returns to its own place in time.' The law of flow means that nothing will ever stay the same. That can be very difficult to handle, especially when change is unexpected, but because of various Universal laws, we will go through failures as well as successes, pain as well as pleasure, misery as well as happiness.

You may feel it's impossible to prepare for this because we never know when we'll be hit by a curveball, but there is a sure-fire way to lessen the impact of the 'bad' rhythms. Don't attach too much importance to anything that is outside your control. Rely on yourself for your happiness and contentment, not other people or things, because they can be unpredictable, but you are always the authentic you, no matter what happens.

This is not easy, especially when emotions are involved. Life can be challenging, but if we can strive for a state of mind where we are calm and focused most of the time when something bad happens, we can start from a more balanced mindset than someone who is living on an emotional roller coaster.

The Principle of Cause and Effect

'Everything happens according to law. Chance is just a law not yet recognized.' Spiritual people do not believe in coincidence. Everything happens for a reason, even if that reason is unclear at the time. Sooner or later, the bigger picture will emerge from the chaos of the situation, and all will make sense.

The main thing to take away from this is that it's better to be the cause than the effect. We as humans are gifted with free will, so we can choose whether to act or react in any circumstances. If you wish to be the master of the situation rather than the victim, then always, always act. Consider your position and the possible consequences of action, then go with your intuition. As long as you approach the situation openly and honestly, your inner knowing will not let you down.

The Principle of Gender

'Everything has its masculine and feminine properties. Gender is in everything.' Cast your mind back to school days, and the dreaded language lessons, where you struggled to work out whether French, Spanish, and Italian nouns were masculine or feminine. Just when you thought you had it right, along with would come that pesky exception that proved the rule.

Like me, you probably wondered how an object could properly be described as either masculine or feminine, and it seems that, at least according to the Hermetic Principles, we had it right. Once again, it's about the balance, and the feminine and masculine qualities of yin and yang, which are complementary and interdependent.

When we can balance the two energies within ourselves, we become more efficient and more knowing. The 'get on with it' male energy is tempered by the more cautious, creative female energy, and more gets done, and done properly.

There, then, are the 7 Hermetic Principles. While you can probably go along with most, if not all of that, you may be wondering how it fits in with Wicca theory, and how you can carry it forward in your life.

Since Aleister Crowley defined magick as 'Creating change according to our will,' it's easy to see the connection with mentalism, the principle that 'The Mind is All.' As Wiccans, because we believe in the concept of The One, we embrace our connection and use it to make change according to our will.

That's just one example of using the principles in Wicca, but in truth, just as everything in the Universe is connected, so are the principles connected in what we do. Think of the 7 Hermetic Principles not just as an ancient doctrine, but a vibrant code of ethics that we can incorporate into our practices, and a tool to help us understand how and why our magick works so well for us. It's basically the Law of Attraction in action before all the wannabe life coaches got their hands on it and reshaped it to suit their purposes and fit into sound bytes in their free e-books.

In this chapter, we've considered in depth many of the theories, principles, and guidelines that underpin Wiccan practice, and two terms have cropped up a lot, although there has been no detailed explanation about them. That's because these topics are so huge, yet so tightly woven through Wicca that they deserve a chapter to themselves.

What are those powerful terms? Energy and the Divine, and in the next chapter, we'll explain about energy and decipher the Divine. After that, you'll have enough theoretical knowledge to be able to move on to the more practical side of Wicca. Blessed Be!

Chapter 3: Energy Explained, and the Divine Deciphered

For centuries, witchcraft and spiritualism have been dismissed as having no bearing on reality, since there can be no scientific proof of the existence of other, non-physical dimensions. Magic was dismissed as mere illusion, okay for entertainment purposes and taking the minds of the masses off their abject poverty for a time, but with no basis in fact.

It's taken a while, but finally, scientists have admitted what spiritual people have always known – everything is energy, and energy can't be destroyed. When the physical body dies, the soul (the body's energy) leaves for another place. In Wicca, we call it Summerland, Christians call it Heaven, Muslims, and Zoroastrians call it Paradise. We know that energy doesn't die, and apparently, so do the scientists now. Let's take a brief look at their evidence before we get back to the witchy stuff.

Quantum Mechanics and the Law of Attraction

There is a distinct relationship between quantum physics, spirituality, thoughts and feelings, and success levels. This connection exists because everything is energy, and energy is constantly shifting.

Around 1850, Rudolf Clausius came up with his First Thermodynamic Law, which stated that 'Energy can neither be created nor destroyed.' It can, however, transform into different forms of energy and redirected. So, where does energy come from, if it's not created? A lot of the energy we use here on Earth actually comes from the sun, and the rest comes from the Earth's molten core, which is made up of iron and nickel and radiates heat at a temperature of 6,000 degrees Celcius. That's 10,800 degrees Fahrenheit, so it's pretty cozy in there!

You can't touch or hold energy since it's a property of matter, which determines the density, and vibrational level of different things around us. There are various forms of energy – kinetic energy, electricity, magnetism, to name but a few. The energy spiritual people work with – spiritual energy – is another form of energy, also known as 'prana,' 'qi,' or the Universal life force. While science has made good progress in terms of identifying and assessing energy as eternal, indestructible energy, it hasn't made much progress with prana, as I like to call it. We'll talk more about that later.

Following on from Albert Einstein's work on energy at the beginning of the 20th century, quantum mechanics has demonstrated that it is possible to create reality simply by observing it. This ties in with the basic tenets of the Law of Attraction, which state that what you put out into the world in thought, word and deed comes back to you. This, in turn, ties in with the Wiccan Law of Threefold Return, where everything you put out, good or bad, returns magnified by three. All is energy, and it isn't love that makes the world go around, as the poets would have us believe, it's energy!

At the core of all this is the scientific fact that light and matter don't exist until they are made real, and it's consciousness that makes things real. In essence, we are the co-creators of our own reality, as we can shape energy particles into what we wish them to be by focusing on our preferred outcome. Conversely, we can ignore the realities we don't like, denying them the opportunity to manifest into our reality. It's all very complex, and as spiritual people, it makes our heads hurt, but we needed to the point that out before moving on to why energy is so important in Wiccan practice.

Harnessing the Power of Energy in Wicca

From the Law of Attraction, we know that positive thoughts and deeds shape our reality, and so do negative ones. It goes without saying, then, that in order to grow spiritually and manifest our best outcomes, we must shift our perspective so that what we put out into the Universe is predominantly positive. We all have down days – we are only human after all – so don't panic if you had a couple of negative thoughts yesterday.

Our negative output only becomes a problem when we focus on it. If we do that, we create a reality that only bad things happen to us, so it's futile to expect positive things to happen when our thought patterns are entrenched in negativity.

Energy is power!

If you've ever seen a flood, either on the television news or in real life, you know that water energy is powerful. If you've seen a tree uprooted in a gale, you know that wind energy is powerful. If you've watched fire devastate the arid plains in Spain in summer, you know that fire energy is powerful. And if like me, you live on a fault line and are often woken by the tremors of an earthquake, although thankfully they are usually mild, then you know that earth energy is powerful.

What you may not realize is that, in its own way, your fifth element energy – your prana – is also very powerful. I'll prove it to you right now.

✔ Sit comfortably in your favorite seat, or cross-legged on the floor, and take a few deep breaths to relax fully.

✔ Place your hands in the conventional 'Prayer' position, palms lightly touching, fingers straight.

✔ Now bring your palms slightly apart and focus your gaze on the gap between them.

✔ Within seconds, you should feel a warmth between your palms, and maybe a tingling sensation as well. That's your own personal prana. Say hello to it if it's your first acquaintance! If you don't feel this, try rubbing your palms together for a few seconds.

✔ Once the energy is flowing, gradually move your hands apart, pulsing them without touching, to build the energy. Each time you can feel the resistance building, widen your hands a little more, until they are 4 – 5 inches apart.

✔ Now form your prana into a ball with your hands. Feel the resistance building even more. Well done!

'This is all very well,' I hear you thinking, 'but what do I do now?' You're going to prove just how powerful the energy you just called up is. Still holding your 'ball,' raise both hands 3 – 4 inches above your head. Now, with a quick downward motion, drop that energy over your head and shoulders.

You'll feel an instant boost of energy, physically and mentally. You can call up that power any time you want to, either to give yourself a boost or to send it to a friend or family member who may need a bit of healing energy. In that case, bring your hands in front of your chest, near your heart, visualize the recipient of your energy and throw it away – in the direction of the main door if you are inside, and just away from you if you are outdoors. See your energy traveling to the intended recipient as a ball of bright green, healing light, which enters his/her chest and fills their body with a glowing green light.

This technique can be used on anyone but do ask their permission first – don't just assume they will welcome it. There may be any number of reasons why they may refuse, and you have to accept that.

When you've been working with energy, drink a glass of water to bring back your awareness to the room, and to hydrate yourself. Energy work can deplete your stores if you don't practice adequate self-care.

Can the power of the mind really heal people and make a difference? Yes, it can, and the more you practice, the more confident you will become in your own abilities.

Scientifically, prayer has been proven to make a difference, even if the recipient didn't know about it. A recent experiment by the University of Maryland Medical Center demonstrated that those who prayed regularly were less likely to suffer from depression and anxiety, had lower blood pressure, was seen to be generally calmer, and even healed from surgery more quickly than those who didn't include regular prayers in their lives.

What is prayer anyway, other than positive energy being sent across space and time? In essence, it's direct communication with The One, the Source, the Divine. It's us opening our hearts with love and respect and being prepared to hand our burdens over, trusting that all will be well. It's an expression of faith, for people of all religions and no religion.

Prayer is an energetic connection with Source and a plea for help. Spellcasting also uses energy, but in a different way. When we pray, we acknowledge the power of whoever we are praying to, and trust that they will help us in a way that will bring about the best possible outcome for all concerned. However, when a spell is cast, the power resides in the witch, who is manipulating energy to make beneficial changes.

Both prayer and spells require energy; it's just the balance of power in that energy that varies. As Wiccans, we can influence and work with energy in other ways than by casting spells or using prayers. Let's take a look at other ways we can harness the energy all around us as part of our practice.

Working with Crystal Energy

Many witches work with crystals, either for self-care, for healing others or for rituals. Crystals are two-way energy sources because they contain their own beneficial energy, which they can then transfer to other people or to us in order to help us make beneficial changes and heal ourselves and others. Meditating with crystals is also beneficial, as you can connect with them for a number of reasons, including finding calmness, courage, forgiveness, clarity of thought, releasing limiting beliefs and ties to the past, and generally raising your vibration.

Carrying a piece of clear quartz around with you will automatically raise your vibration, while amethyst will help enhance your spiritual powers as well as raising your vibrations and keeping you focused on unconditional love. There is literally a crystal for everything, and in most cases, there are several to choose from.

The power of crystals is scientifically proven – clear quartz gives clarity of thought and is able to store an enormous amount of data. It's the storage properties of clear quartz that allow me to write this book so quickly and allow you to read it so easily. If quartz is capable of holding so much energy, just imagine how many good, healing intentions, you can program into it!

The shape of the crystals has a bearing on their energetic power too, and this was proven by legendary IBM research scientist Marcel Vogel, who passed to Spirit in 1991. Vogel proved that the naturally occurring hexagonal shapes in crystals amplified the flow and strength of Universal life force energy through the crystals, and he developed the Vogel healing wands, expanding on the omnipresent sacred geometry at the heart of all crystals.

Vogel proved that, if the crystal was programmed with loving intent, many things were possible. In his final years, he had serious heart problems, and at one stage astounded his physician by healing himself to a degree which medical science deemed impossible. That just shows you the true power of energy used lovingly and wisely, doesn't it?

Wear crystals as jewelry, carry them in a pocket, or set them on your altar. When I do moon rituals, I love to incorporate selenite into the ritual. This crystal is closely connected with lunar phases – the name comes from Selene, the Greek goddess of the moon. Selenite has a gentle yet powerful energy and can be used for relaxation and also boosting energy. It's also both cleansing and protective, so it's a great all-round crystal for maintaining your sacred space.

Crystals can also be used as powerful additions to spells and rituals and working with them is an excellent way to harness the energy of the Universe simply and safely. Let the crystals choose you – it's much better to go to a shop or mind, body spirit fair rather than order your crystals online.

You need to handle them and connect with the energy. Like us, each crystal is individual, and the energy varies. You will connect with some, and not with others, even if they are all the same crystal. It's a bit like going into a room full of people who belong to the same club and have the same interests as you. Some you will be drawn to, and others will not make much of an impression. The relationship you build with your crystals is like building a friendship with someone you relate to as soon as you meet, so don't rush it, and don't allow anyone else to influence your decisions.

Working with Intention

Another way you can work with energy is to practice intention. This can work with crystals – when you acquire a new crystal, you may decide you want to work with it in a certain way, so you will sit quietly with it in meditation and program your intent into the crystal. If anyone tells you it's impossible to program crystals, just remind them that if it were, they wouldn't be using their tablets, smartphones and other electronic devices, because they are all powered by microchips, which are ... programmed crystals!

Alternatively, you can use the intention process to rewrite the script of your day if it starts badly. For example, you may feel obliged to attend a family gathering that you really don't want to go to, but you know if you don't, your Mom will be really upset.

Instead of telling yourself you wish you could be anywhere else in the world, set the intention to enjoy your day. Visualize yourself looking forward to spending quality time with family members you don't see very often, enjoying the drive to the event, maybe stopping off to take photos of the fabulous views on the way. Decide how you are going to dress, so you feel good and make your Mom proud of you – you're doing this for her sake, after all.

Because you have put out so much positivity about the dreaded family gathering, you will have a great time, because what you put out comes back. If you expect to be bored out of your brain, rest assured you will be, so make sure all your thoughts about the family gathering are positive.

To complete the intention process, be sure to practice gratitude. Thank the Universe for bringing all the elements together so that you, your family, and your close friends could make the most of this special time together.

The intention setting technique can be applied to just about any situation, and as you become more familiar with it, it will become easier to shift your energy focus. It's all about energy – always!

Working with Cleansing Energy

As we know, energy can be good or bad, positive or negative. What you may not realize is that you have the power to purify and banish negative or bad energy, and there are several ways you can do this. The most commonly used method is smudging using herbs.

The term smudging refers to any cleansing and clearing method that uses smoke as a purifier – it doesn't mean you need to cover everything with ash from sage sticks, or whatever herb you happen to use. I mention sage because white sage is the herb most associated with smudging, but herbs such as lavender, sweetgrass, and frankincense can also be used. It doesn't need to be herb sticks either – it's the smoke that's important, so incense sticks or cones will work just as well as tailor-made smudging sticks.

As we keep saying, all is energy, and herbs have their energetic correspondences too, so what you use may depend on the energies you are clearing. If you want to restore harmony after a relationship breaks up or a family row, choose lavender for smudging, as it restores inner peace and clears the energy of the conflict from the air.

For personal cleansing auras or healing spaces of negative energy, try sweetgrass. Smudging with sage will purify your home and cleanse and empower healing crystals. It's also helpful if someone in the family has asthma or allergies. Frankincense is good for relieving stress and tension, in people or in the home, and it can also relieve headaches and other aches and pains precipitated by tension.

To smudge successfully, it's not just a matter of lighting a stick and waving it around until someone gets annoyed and tells you to stop. It's a sacred, spiritual ceremony, so ensure you are calm and relaxed and focus your intent on what you wish to achieve with the smudging. It could be inner peace for yourself, conflict resolution for someone close, or maybe you've had a negative person in the house, and they've left behind stagnant energy that is affecting the sensitive members of the household.

Take some deep, relaxing breaths, then light your smudge tool and wait for it to smoke. Use your hand or a large feather - which has been held in the smoke beforehand to cleanse it – to waft the smoke where it needs to go. When you feel all the negativity has been moved on, thank the Universe for helping you to cleanse your space and ask that all negative energies are sent to Mother Earth to be cleansed, transmuted and returned to the Universe as love, with love.

This last step is more important than you may think. As we know, energy cannot be destroyed. However, if it is not cleansed and transmuted once it has left our space, it will remain as negative energy, and we will have merely passed the problem to someone else to deal with. That serves nobody, so we need to ask for transmutation so that we can do our bit to raise the vibrations around us.

Make smudging a regular part of your spiritual practice, so that you can assist the Universe in clearing the prevailing energies. When we do something good for the Universe, we help everyone and everything, because we are all part of The One, and that in turn raises our own vibration.

Energy is such a vast and interesting topic, I could write for hours and still only scratch at the surface, so it's time to move on. However, if you want to learn more about how energy works, and how we can harness it to further our spiritual growth and help others, there is plenty of research material around, in print and online. Let's talk now about the other major influence on Wiccan theory and practice – the relationship with the Divine.

Wiccans Working with the Divine

The common dictionary definition of the word 'divine' is 'Of a god, godlike.' And here's the first place we see a discrepancy in the divine as a general concept and the Divine in Wicca. The definition mentions god, which is a male assignment, whereas, in Wicca, the male and female elements of the Divine are equally important, because Wicca is not based on patriarchy, but on equality. Indeed, when we speak of our deities, it's customary to refer to 'the Goddess and the God,' rather than place God first.

The double deities have correspondences with other ancient gods and goddesses – for example, the Goddess with Diana, Artemis, and Isis, to name but a few, and the God with Pan, Cernunnos, and Herne. However, it's traditional in Wicca not to name them, as they each embody characteristics from members of the whole pantheon that has gone before them. Some solitary practitioners and covens may give names to the Goddess and the God to give them a more personal association, but if they do, they tend to keep their associations to themselves.

The God is associated with the sun, the Earth as protector and action, while the Goddess is connected with the moon, the Earth as nurturer, and emotions. They are represented on Wicca altars and honored in major rites and magic rituals.

The Goddess and the God are celebrated in Wicca as two equal energy forces, masculine and feminine, each a part of the whole, and each a part of the Universe, therefore it's not necessary to identify them separately by name. That said, some Wiccan traditions – notably the Dianic Wiccans –only recognize and worship the goddess Diana.

The whole Goddess and God issue are further complicated for beginners since the Wiccan flexibility of belief mean followers are free to worship a particular deity of their own choice, or they could even be drawn to a deity with whom they already share a number of spiritual connections. This could be an Egyptian deity like Isis or Ra, the Norse goddess Freya, or the Celtic god Herne. If someone is genuinely drawn to a particular deity, according to Wiccan teaching, it is right that they choose to work with them.

Nevertheless, in practice, the chosen deities will often still be identified as the Goddess or the God, or maybe the Lady or the Lord, and that's how confusion arises. Wicca is a flexible religion, and its practitioners enjoy the freedom to worship any god and goddess who calls to them spiritually. These deities may belong to any religion and any pantheon, not just Wiccan and pagan tradition. Many Wiccans believe that naming gods, or even identifying them as masculine and feminine, is irrelevant to spiritual practice anyway.

As a newcomer to Wicca, you may find it simpler to begin your practice using the concept of the Triple Goddess and the Horned God. As you progress on your path, you may or may not be called to specific deities. The essential thing is to be sincere in your interactions and believe in the power of your own divinity and the divinity of the essence of that which you worship.

A major tenet of Wicca is the understanding that there is a spark of divinity in everyone and everything. Nature is divine, as well as all the products of Nature – the plants, the animals, the waters, the Earth, the sky, the mountains, and of course, ourselves. We are all connected to

The One, and to Everything That Is and therein resides our personal divinity.

The One is essentially the all-inclusive unity of everything that has ever existed. This takes in all that exists as restricted human knowledge, as well as everything that is no longer or has never been embodied. One is frankly immeasurable, and it is pretty much impossible to begin to comprehend its immensity. Wiccans, being practical as well as spiritual beings, don't even bother to try!

Whether we think of The One as the Universe, the Creator, one God or several combined is irrelevant to Wiccan belief. We are all connected to The One, and all our thoughts, words, and deeds have far-reaching effects, way beyond the reach of our personal circle. Therefore we must consider our actions and take full responsibility for them, always.

If you've been paying attention so far, you should have a pretty good grasp of Wiccan theory, and you're itching to get into the Wiccan way of life. Hopefully, this hasn't been too confusing for you, and there hasn't been information overload. The thing about Wicca is, there is no fixed doctrine, which is great when you want to express your spiritual individuality, but not so good when you're just setting out.

In the next chapter, we'll talk about living the Wiccan way, and whether you want to work as a solitary practitioner or would prefer to be initiated into a coven. We'll also take a brief look at the most popular and well-known traditions of Wicca, to help you refine your choices and make the decisions that are right for you. This is, after all, your journey. Blessed Be!

Chapter 4: Living the Wiccan Way

Being a Wiccan is not something you are normally born into. You discovered Wicca by chance unless you belong to a family of practicing Wiccans. Newcomers to Wicca often find that they view Nature in exactly the same way as they did before they learned about Wicca because an affinity with Nature is often one of the things that draw people to this religion.

Wicca is more than just a religion; it's a way of life. It's not about going to church on Sundays then forgetting about it the rest of the week, having done what was expected of you. In fact, for Wiccans, their church is wherever they feel best able to connect with Nature, the Universe, and Everything That Is, and that's normally outdoors. A forest, a cliff top, a beach, a riverbank – anywhere is suitable for Wiccan worship and ritual.

You get to decide what works for you and what fits with your beliefs. The first decision you need to make is whether you prefer to work as a solitary practitioner, or as an initiate in a coven. Let's take a look at the pros and cons of each way of working. Personally, I like to fly solo – it's also the most practical choice for me right now, but we are all different, and how you choose to follow your Wiccan path is entirely up to you.

Solo Practitioner or Member of a Coven?

As I just stated, I like to work alone, as do most of the Wiccan friends I know about, but others like the discipline, tradition, and sense of fellowship that belonging to a coven provides. It's really down to personal choice, and how you see your spiritual journey unfolding. The obvious advantage of practicing as a solo is that your Wiccan path can be absolutely personal and unique, which is how Wicca rocks. That said if you are nervous about taking those first steps on the Wiccan Way, you may want to join a coven.

A coven is often a great place to hone and develop your craft, make new, like-minded friends, and become involved in wonderful Wiccan experiences. Problems can arise if you happen to select a coven that's unsuitable for your requirements, or if you are drawn into a coven with substandard spiritual practices. This could create negative energy within yourself, which in turn may have a detrimental effect on your developing powers. You could become severely depressed as a result, at the very time when you should be joyfully celebrating the development of your powers.

It's invariably better to get the negative stuff out of the way first, and then look forward with positivity. These are some reasons why a particular coven may not be the right spiritual fit for you. If any of these resonate, reconsider your decision right away.

Remember, Wicca is a philosophy that is, above all else, flexible and adaptable to your personal spiritual needs. If anyone insists that their way of working is the only true Wiccan way, or if they ask you not to work with resources they don't endorse, step away. None of us is perfect – we are human, after all - and some people can get a little drunk on personal power and demand unquestioning obedience from coven members. This conduct is diametrically opposed to the essential spirit and understanding of Wiccan belief, and it is not the way to take your initial, perhaps faltering, steps along your chosen spiritual path.

Be cautious if anyone tries to coerce you into nudity or behavior of a sexual nature. Some Wiccan traditions do perform rituals naked – notably the Gardnerians. However, the Wiccan way is not about control of any description.

Public or private humiliation of coven members is also in violation of the Wiccan Rede directive 'Harm None.'

Magic is more powerful than most people comprehend, and anyone attempts to use it to cause harm or control others, they abuse the infinite blessings of the Universe. Be wary of anyone who tries to force you to remain in a coven if you are not getting spiritual benefit from belonging. If you haven't undergone initiation into a coven after some time, then you are not an official member of that coven. Initiation usually takes place one year and one day following your first introduction to a coven.

Briefly, anyone who denies your right to freedom of thought, or tries to intimidate, threaten or frighten you is best avoided, both in life and in Wicca. They cannot be authentic Wiccans since they show no respect for or love for Wicca or its practitioners.

So then, what makes a good coven? The most altruistic coven members and teachers will all be decent men and women at heart, and this quality will shine through in their conduct. A gifted teacher will happily answer your questions – and will almost certainly encourage them. Wicca is about experience and knowledge, and to learn more, you will need to ask questions. If in doubt, trust your intuition. If you are comfortable around a teacher or mentor, it's more than likely they will be good for your spiritual growth.

Many people start on the Wiccan Way by researching, reading, and teaching themselves. Some may take online courses to reinforce their knowledge. They may then work as solitary practitioners before they consider joining a coven if they ever do. It's not a requirement of Wicca, and only you can decide if your experience will be enhanced by belonging to a coven.

If you decide this is a wise option for you, take time to get to know other initiates if you can. Some covens can be rather secretive, so that may not be possible. Never seem as if you are desperate to join a coven, even if you can't wait! Such conduct could attract the wrong kind of people to you, as you may come across as needy. Trust your gut instinct in all things – it won't let you down.

Coven Size

Traditionally, there have always been 13 witches in a coven, including the High Priestess and the High Priest. There are various theories on why it should be so, but the two most popular explanations seem to be that it is because there are 13 full moons in the year, or that 13 people are the most that can be comfortably accommodated in a 9-foot diameter ritual circle.

In practice, Wiccan covens can be smaller or larger, with as few as four members – or coveners, as they are called – or 20 or more. These days, it is rare to find Wiccan covens numbering more than between 13 or 20, because when that number is reached, the coven leaders tend to create satellite covens, which meet up at the major sabbats. The reason for keeping the numbers down is so that all coveners can take turns at the different ritual tasks that are performed at each gathering, thus increasing their knowledge and experience.

Another reason for keeping coven size manageable is so that the coveners can build close relationships with their fellows. It can get a bit impersonal if too many people are involved.

Let's now take a look at the various Wicca traditions, to help you decide if one of the divisions of Wicca is more suitable for your spiritual expression than others. This is not an exhaustive list, just a summary of the main aspects of the most popular traditions.

Wiccan Traditions

We know that Wicca is a relatively new religion – modern Wicca as we understand it today is less than 100 years old, which, in terms of religious culture, is pretty much a newborn! That said, many of the teachings and practices of Wicca have their roots in ancient, pre-Christian pagan religions. Some aspects of Wiccan practice are common to all traditions, but there are also distinct differences. You may feel that a particular tradition leaves you cold, while a different one could be a perfect spiritual fit for you. Your individual soul journey may even cross over more than one tradition. Here's a summary of the key points of the more well-known Wicca traditions to guide you in your choice.

Gardnerian Tradition

The Gardnerian Wiccan tradition can be defined as both a tradition and a family, and a High Priestess leads the coven, ensuring that love, trust, and honesty preside over all the activities. Wiccans do not have an official sacred text, but there is *The Book of Shadows*. Originally devised by Gerald Gardner, the founder of modern Wicca, the original volume has been handed down through generations. Gardnerian Wiccans are free to adapt and adopt other rites and add to *The Book of Shadows*, provided they preserve the original volume.

Gardnerian Wiccans tend to worship naked – or skyclad, as they call it. They practice binding and scourging, are very hierarchal, and also secretive. For these reasons, they are the most controversial of all Wiccan traditions and are the first Wiccan tradition to be accepted in the United States of America.

The Gardnerian covens each independent of others and are led by a High Priestess. If she should need guidance, she will consult the High Priestess who initiated her. This way of operating means each coven has a formal lineage, which is able to produce proficient and experienced leaders and guides to ensure the continuity of the coven and establish a heritage of tradition and practice.

The two most important doctrines in the Gardnerian tradition are reincarnation and the Wiccan Rede. Most covens typically pair an experienced male and female together to work to create balance. Much of the energy produced in Gardnerian covens is invoked by manifesting the Goddess and the God by means of dancing, chanting, and performing other activities to raise the vibration and connect.

More information about the Gardnerian Wiccan tradition has been published than the rest of the traditions combined. However, the way it operates remains an enigma in the Wiccan world largely.

Alexandrian Tradition

The Alexandrian Tradition shares several similarities with Gardnerian Wicca. However, while the Gardnarian tradition requires complete nudity for rituals, it is optional in Alexandrian practice. Alexandrian Wiccans tend to use a wand as a symbol of the element of air, and a ceremonial athame as the representation of the fire element. Rites are formal and often include ceremonial magic. Alexandrian Wicca emphasizes male and female polarity, particularly as it relates to sexuality.

The Alexandrian ritual year is shared between the Holly Lord and the Oak Lord, with rites featuring the recurring theme of the dying, then resurrected God. As with Gardnerian Wiccans, Alexandrians also have a High Priestess in charge of the coven. That said, at the time of writing, the main spokespersons for both traditions have always been male!

This tradition was founded by Alex Sanders and his wife, Maxine. He maintained that his grandmother had initiated him into Wicca the early 1930s before it became mainstream. The main ambassadors of Alexandrian Wicca were Janet and Stewart Fararr, whose books are very detailed and informative. The term 'Alexandrian' is not taken from Alex Sanders's name – it's a reference to Alexandria in Ancient Egypt.

As already mentioned, there are a number of similarities and overlaps between Gardnarian and Alexandrian Wicca. However, Alexandrian Wicca is more informal and more liberal, allowing coven members more spiritual flexibility.

Dianic Tradition

There are two main aspects of the Dianic Tradition. The first was established by

Zsuzsanna Budapest at the summer solstice of 1971 and is sometimes referred to as Feminist Dianic Witchcraft. It concentrates on the Goddess herself – though not necessarily Diana, but all aspects of the Goddess as a woman - and only female, women-born-women members are permitted in the covens.

This division of Wicca is not rigorously organized, and they perform simple rituals. Many members are political feminists, but the founder of the tradition simply wanted to establish a pagan spirituality model that was not patriarchal in its organization. There is a strong lesbian presence, but the covens welcome all women, regardless of their sexual orientation.

The second aspect of Dianic Wicca was founded by Morgan McFarland and Mark Roberts, in Texas, USA, soon after McFarland was inspired by a meeting with Budapest at a pagan festival. The Goddess is once again the principal deity in this tradition, and it is heavily influenced by Celtic mythology. It acknowledges the male/female duality and pays homage to the Horned God as the Divine Consort of the Goddess. Both men and women are welcome in this tradition, and there are numerous covens in Texas. These covens are not connected to the original coven of the mid-1970s, so there is no element of continued lineage.

Georgian Tradition

Georgian Wicca is both eclectic and traditional. Material given to new members can technically be referred to as Alexandrian, and there are elements of other traditions, including Gardnerian and Celtic. Some rituals are similar to those of British Traditional Witchcraft (BTW), and teaching is passed from male to female and female to male. Georgian Wicca, like its founder, can be irreverent at times and encourages individuality and creativity in its initiates.

It's a modern tradition, founded in 1970 in California by George Pattison, or 'Pat,' as he is still fondly remembered by his followers. He passed in 1984, and was most famous for saying, 'If it works, then use it if it doesn't, then don't.' The Georgian Wicca newsletter often features advice and information from practitioners of all traditions, and there are covens across many American states.

These are the best known of the Wiccan traditions, and certainly the most structured, as far as Wicca is structured, given the degree of flexibility available to its practitioners. Other traditions you may wish to research further include British Traditional Wicca, which is actually a mixed bag that means different things to different people, depending on their location. I felt the information about it was a little confusing even for me to process, let alone newcomers to Wicca, so I left that one out.

Eclectic Wicca is another tradition that means different things to different people. Then there is Celtic Wicca, based around Celtic myth and tradition, and Erisian Wicca, which takes an opposite view to traditional Wicca, by working on the principle that chaos is just as necessary for worship as order. There's a lot of humor among the more spiritual experiences, and practitioners worship Eris, the Greek goddess of discord.

Now you have some idea of whether you wish to work as a solitary practitioner or a covener, and maybe find yourself drawn to one of the Wicca traditions, let's get down to the practicalities. We've mentioned spells and rituals a few times, and soon we'll go into more detail about these kingpins of Wiccan practice. However, before we do that, we need to make it clear how Wiccan magic works, what it is, and just as importantly, what it is not. To be a successful spell caster, you need to know what you are doing, and why, and in the next chapter, we'll bring you up to speed on Wiccan magic. Blessed Be!

Chapter 5: The Basics of Wiccan Magic

Wiccan magic is not supernatural, nor does it require sleight of hand or 'smoke and mirrors' illusion. That's more accurately described as conjuring, and it's performed for entertainment purposes, rather than life enhancement. Wiccan magic is not magic wands, flashes and bangs and 'Abracadabra.' That stuff belongs in the movies, not in real life.

For practicing Wiccans, magic is a natural and normal aspect of ordinary life. It's all around us, all the time, yet most people never notice it, because they are not expecting to find it! Real-life magic is more a matter of subtle transformation. The root of the term Wicca comes from an ancient derivation of the word 'wic,' meaning 'shape or bend.' That's where the true focus of Wiccan magic lies – it's a reshaping of available Universal energy in order to bring about improvements in areas of your life, or maybe in the lives of your nearest and dearest, whether they are believers or not.

It's not necessary to practice magic to live a Wiccan life, but lots of people do. They believe magic enhances and amplifies their spiritual experiences. Wiccans view their magic as totally different from other traditions of witchcraft, believing it to be spirituality motivated in its intention and execution. As is the case with other Wiccan practices, magic is always performed with due deference to the exhortation in the Wiccan Rede to 'Harm None.'

There is no specialized training, or even the requirement for particular tools in order to practice Wicca magic. Everything you require is inside you; focused intent, the sincere belief that what you want will manifest in your life, and a pure, loving heart. If these essential ingredients are in place, your enchantments and spells are going to work, no danger.

Wiccan magic works exceedingly well in certain sections of your life. Health and wellness, personal security, relationships, social mobility, and financial stability are just some areas where magic can make a difference to you and those close to you. Wiccan magic works mainly by channeling and reshaping the energy around you. Now you know why we went into so much detail when we discussed energy a couple of chapters back!

Magic often works better for the practitioner than for others, and there's a really good reason why that is the case. A supreme, almost superhuman is required to cast a spell or conduct a ritual. This naturally focuses on the spell caster's energy and thinking on the changes the magic needs to bring about. This can result in subtle, non-magical changes in the person's demeanor and thought processes, which helps to facilitate the true intention behind the magic. Wiccan magic is essentially a complex process, creating subtle yet significant changes due to the powerful energies the practitioner calls in.

Some witches like spells to prayers, but Wiccans tend to make a clear distinction between prayers and magic. For Wiccans, prayer is a respectful request. Magic, although similarly respectful in its execution, is more like a command, reinforced with the conscious exercise of will to bring about beneficial change. You need to be in the right frame of mind to perform magic, whereas it's possible to pray at any time, in any place. That's the fundamental difference, in the eyes of Wiccans, between prayers and magic.

An important element of all Wiccan magic is to introduce yourself to the Goddess and the God before asking for their assistance. In Wiccan practice, the pantheon of pagan deities all finds embodiment within the Goddess and the God. There is no requirement to invoke a named deity unless you feel a particular affinity or consider a specific god or goddess can empower your magic. All the gods and goddesses our ancestors worshipped are embodied in The One, who is the supreme being of power, and Everything That Is.

However, etiquette dictates that you identify yourself to The One as a precursor to making your petition for change. After all, you wouldn't approach a stranger in the street and ask for help without so much as a 'Hello,' so why would you behave like that with the Goddess and the God? It's only polite to introduce yourself.

Your work with magic is best kept to yourself - particularly if those closest to you are not Wiccan practitioners. Of course, you are confident of the power of your magic, but others may dismiss it as so much nonsense. That could generate waves of negative energy, which could prevent your spell from working as you expect it to.

Wiccan magic works for the highest good for all concerned, so it can never be invoked to interfere with the free will of anyone else. You cannot use magic to cause your crush to fall in love with you if there is no mutual attraction to start with. Sometimes, the magic may apparently fail because the result you want is not what you actually need at that time.

The Goddess and the God can see the bigger picture, which is denied to the rest of us. They are aware of all the possible outcomes, as well as any potential hindrances to success, so your magic may surprise you by working in ways you never even considered. Rest assured, you will always have the best outcome for your highest good and happiness.

Always maintain total focus and concentration when working with magic. If stray thoughts work their way into your mind, send them on their way, or your magic will not work. Have confidence and faith in everything you do and trust your skills. Know that you can do it! I find meditation helps to clear my mind of chatter before I work with magic. It's worth trying it for yourself – or you could color a mandala to use as a focal point in your spell. Adult coloring is a form of meditation in itself since you must shut out everything from your mind in order to concentrate on the delicate patterns of the mandalas.

Some forms of magic work with variations on affirmations to help people reach their goals.

This simple technique is a great practice for newcomers to Wicca. Think of a word or a short phrase that is a perfect summary of whatever it is you would like to achieve. Write your word or phrase ten times each day, on a fresh sheet of paper, until you have brought about the change you require. You might decide to write, 'I am Wiccan, and I transform my life with my magic.' As you write, visualize it happening for you now, and focus on making it happen. You can do this at any time, in any place, and it may only take a few days for you to achieve your desires.

There is nothing out of the ordinary about Wiccan magic since the energy to perform it is freely available for anyone to make use of, in the right way, for the right reasons. People outside Wicca do not comprehend how powerful magic can be and how easy it is to cast spells to improve your life. Magic need not be complicated in order to work– it's as simple – and as complex – as having the right touch, from the right person, with the right intent.

Now we've established that Wiccan magic is simply using ordinary tools, rituals, and words to bring about extraordinary transformations, it's time to take a closer look at the ceremonial side of Wiccan practice. There are certain rituals that are the exclusive preserve of the Wiccan religion, while others have been adapted from ancient pagan traditions.

To avoid information overload, we're just going to talk about the essential practices that are used in almost everything we do. There's a whole other book to be written on Wiccan rituals, and there are many out there you can check on if you wish. However, the main idea behind this book is to provide a beginners' guide and get you working the Wiccan Way as quickly as possible. There'll be plenty of time for research later. Blessed Be!

Chapter 6: Essential Wiccan Rituals

We live our lives according to various rituals to give structure, meaning, and purpose to our existence. The dictionary defines ritual as 'A religious or sacred ceremony consisting of a number of defined actions performed in a prescribed order,' and that's where Wiccan ritual differs from our daily routine. The sky won't fall in if you shower before breakfast rather than after, as usual. However, sacred rituals are developed over the years in specific ways, in order to bring about beneficial change, protection, or to clear negative energies and create a sacred space where everyone feels safe.

Rituals are normally associated with landmark moments, in particular births, deaths, initiations, and hind castings. The various reasons for conducting them may be to bring joy, ease grief or sorrow, or just to celebrate with like-minded people. Rituals are, by definition, repetitive, and the same sequence of actions is carried out every time the ritual is performed since people find security and comfort in the familiar.

Wiccan ritual practice requires the participants to reflect and consider what they are doing and clarify what they expect to accomplish with the assistance of the ritual. This mindful reflection helps the practitioner focus their intent on the true purpose and meaning of the ritual they are about to enact.

Wiccans and pagans have always believed that rituals should be conducted outdoors if at all possible, to emphasize the divine connection that Wicca enjoys with Nature. There is no need for special buildings, as practitioners prefer to conduct rituals in outdoor spaces like caves, hillsides, riverbanks, woods, cliff tops. Even private gardens and terraces can be used as the setting for Wiccan rituals since the most powerful connections with the Goddess are usually achieved outdoors.

In short, a Wiccan ritual can be performed anywhere the practitioner chooses. A consecrated building such as a church, chapel, or temple is not necessary, because the area where the ritual will take place is routinely cleansed and purified before the sacred circle is marked out.

The sacred circle has been mentioned a few times, and it is an essential component of any ritual – whether it is intended for casting spells, divination work, working with energy, or anything else a Wiccan practitioner may care to carry out. Let's take a close look at the elements of casting a sacred circle and discover why it is such an essential feature of Wiccan practice.

Casting the Sacred Circle and Calling the Quarters

The sacred and infinite circle, where everyone is safe and equal as they work, is a cornerstone of Wiccan practice. Before starting to cast the circle, the area where it will be drawn is ceremoniously cleansed and purified with a broom.

This broom – or besom – is an iconic symbol of Wicca and witchcraft. However, it has a practical purpose as well, as it is used to sweep away negative energies literally. It's customary to start and finish the ritual sweeping near a door, so any residual negative energies can be swept outside. Besoms used for ceremonial cleansing should be kept for that purpose only and should never be used for regular house cleaning. This is a sacred tool after all, and if it was used for other purposes, it could attract more negative energies, which would defeat the object of the ritual cleansing.

To cast the circle, begin at either the North or the East point, and walk in a circular direction deosil (clockwise). While walking, mark out the boundaries of the circle, or visualize it, using a wand as you go. You can physically mark out the circle by sprinkling salt – for further cleansing - as you walk, or drawing a line in the earth with a stick, or the circle can just be visualized. It's down to personal preference, really.'

Place Elemental Candles in position at the quarters of the circle, which corresponds to the main compass points.

Now invite each of the four main Elements to enter the circle and 'Be present and watch over the circle.' The wording for this invocation can be a personal choice, so say what your intuition advises The Element of Spirit is now called on, before the Goddess and the God are invited in. The sacred circle is a protected space between the worlds of Earth and Spirit. Negative energies and dark powers have no place here, so the practitioner/s are always safe and secure as they do their work.

Once the ceremonials are concluded, it's customary to thank the Elements and the

Goddess and the God for being present. Finally, close the sacred circle by walking widdershins (anti-clockwise), using your wand to visualize the closing of the circle.

The sacred circle is used by all Wiccan practitioners, whether working alone or within a coven. Coven circles are traditionally around 9 feet wide, to accommodate all the coveners and their ritual tools, and allow for the safe movement of athames and chalices during the proceedings.

Drawing Down the Moon

This is one of the most important rituals and spiritual practices in Wicca, and it's enacted at the time of the Full Moon. There are two distinct purposes to this ritual. The first is to draw down the light and energy of the Full Moon, and fill oneself with Divine Light, thereby strengthening the connection with the Divine that Wiccans believe is within us all.

Drawing Down the Moon is an empowering ritual that can help with healing, and overcome depression, fear, negative feelings, and lack of self-esteem. You can perform this ritual through visualization, but it is so much better to carry it out when you are actually facing the moon, outdoors.

Offer a greeting and a gift, then ask for the help you need, while stating what kind of energy you wish to call down. Adopt the Chalice position – with your arms raised above your head in a cupped, Y-shaped position resembling a receptive chalice. Clap your hands once over your head, then return to the Chalice position. Visualize the Moon pouring brilliant light into your chalice and hold that vision for a few seconds.

Lower your arms slowly, drawing down the light from your chalice into every part of your body and soul. Feel it flooding into you and experience it all with your senses. Repeat this action at least three times more – and remember to clap. It helps to focus your full intent on the ritual. It's common to feel tingling and buzzing after this, and also to feel a sense of disorientation, due to the power of the energy you have just drawn down. Sit down on the earth until you get your balance back and drink some water to ground you again.

In my own version of drawing down the moon, I use a selenite unicorn horn and hold it over my head. Once the energy has entered the crystal, I sweep the horn over my main chakra points and visualize the moon energy pouring into every cell of my body.

A further variation is to take a glass of water outside with you when you prepare for your ritual. Imagine the moon's silver light pouring into the water as you hold the glass high. Now drink the water down, and see it flood through your body, taking the silver light with it. Center the energy in your sacral chakra, and hold it there, to be slowly released over the waning phase of the moon.

When your ritual is completed, thank the Moon for filling you with her Divine Light and energy. You may kiss your hand to honor her, make a namaste bow, or come up with your own way to honor and thank the Moon for her help.

The second way of drawing down the moon is not really for beginners since it involves invoking the Goddess and allowing her to channel messages and advice through you, either in her voice or yours. More often than not, this ritual is conducted by the High Priestess of a coven or a very experienced solitary practitioner. It can be overwhelming and even a little scary, so it's not something to approach lightly.

The Great Rite

While casting a circle and drawing down the moon is the most familiar of Wiccan rituals, there is another aspect of ritual that has been sensationalized over time, and that is ritual sex. For many years, there was a false perception that witches continuously engaged in all kinds of debauchery, including nudity, group sex, and even sex with demons and Satan himself. Much of this stemmed from the middle ages when the persecution of alleged witches was prevalent, and people could pretty much say anything they wanted about suspected witches.

The truth of the matter is, although ritual sex is part of Wiccan practice, it doesn't mean that coven members routinely have sex. It can be symbolic, where the male symbol of the athame is placed in the receptive female chalice. Or there may just be a build-up of sexual energy. If actual sex takes place during a ritual, it will be between consenting adults, and will mostly take place in private rather than in public.

The Great Rite honors the balance of masculine and feminine in The One and recreates the birth of the Universe. Gerald Gardner, the founder of modern Wicca, envisioned Wicca as a fertility religion above all else, so it follows that there would be some reference to sacred sex, whether it is symbolic or actual. The Great Rite is also symbolic of the union of the practitioner with Nature and the Cosmos as another aspect and recreation of The One.

Sexual energy – including masturbation – is a valid Wiccan method of raising energy. And male and female energy does not necessarily mean you need a male and a female to perform the Great Rite since aspects of the male and the female reside in all of us. Pagan ritual sex practices were established at a time when people were unaware that 'it takes two to tango,' so to speak, and women were revered as akin to goddesses for their ability to recreate human life. Fertile females were revered by their tribes for as long as they were able to produce new life, and then a younger female would assume the role of the 'goddess in the tribe.

These days, if ritual sex is performed, it's more likely to be symbolic rather than literal, and it's not as common as it was previously. One time when the Great Rite is likely to be enacted is at the sabbat of Beltane, on 1 May, when spring is in the air, and it's all about rebirth.

Whether you participate in the Great Rite or other sacred sex rituals is entirely a matter of personal choice. Since sex is seen as a sacred act in Wicca, there should be no pressure on anyone who is uncomfortable with this type of ritual to take part, whether the sex is symbolic or otherwise. Certainly, there should never be any hint of coercion or intimidation to force coveners to participate in rituals against their will.

These, then, are some of the core rituals of Wiccan practice, and you are likely to come across one or more of them on a frequent basis. As with all things Wicca, nothing is cast in stone, and you can adapt these rituals to suit your personal preferences and interests.

Experienced Wiccans advise everyone to conduct all spells, rituals, and acts of magic from the safety and sanctity of the sacred circle. Ensure you are familiar with all the aspects of the ritual you wish to conduct before attempting it, and make sure you have any tools or other items ready before you begin. Once you are in full swing of the ritual, the last thing you want to have to do is start over because you've forgotten a vital element of the ritual. Above all, enjoy the rituals of your spiritual practice, and remember, all is flexible in Wicca, so, by all means, edit and adapt the rituals to suit your personal preferences.

Before we leave this topic and move on to actual spell casting, there's one more consideration you should be aware of, and it's something you may not have even thought about. The way you prepare for and perform rituals is at least as important as the reason for conducting them.

You should be clean in body, and pure of thought and intention, so the energy can flow freely to enable the magic to do its work. Take a shower or a ritual bath in preparation, and at this point, you may wish to anoint your body with suitable oil to help build the right energy for what you wish to accomplish, or to forge a stronger connection during your ritual. Oils can also be used on your altar, crystals, and ritual tools such as wands, chalices, athames, and crystals. For instance, when communing with the Goddess in rituals, you may wish to use frankincense or wisteria oil, since both are very spiritual, and promote a stronger connection with the Divine. We'll look more deeply into magical correspondences in the next chapter.

Meditate to clear your mind, clarify your thoughts, and direct your intent to the ritual. Take your time and spend as much time as you feel is necessary on every element of the ritual. At the end of the ceremony, remember to thank and honor the Elements, the Goddess and the God, the Moon, and any other powers you may have called on during the course of the ritual. Above all, enjoy the experience – Wicca rituals are designed to be enjoyed rather than endured. Wicca is primarily a religion of peace, love, and joy, and these elements of Wicca should be adequately reflected in your rituals.

With each chapter of this book, you are learning more about the theory and practice of Wicca, and now I'm going to show you how to cast some basic spells to encourage you to make full use of your developing Wiccan powers to make beneficial changes in your own life and maybe help your friends and family members. Welcome to the wonderful world of Wicca. Blessed Be!

Chapter 7: Some Basic Wiccan Spells to Try

While many non-Wiccans may assume that magic and spell casting is at the heart of the Wiccan practice, it's actually secondary to the spiritual and religious elements of Wicca. That said, magic and spells are integral to the Wiccan practice, and while you don't need to practice magic to be a Wiccan, many Wiccans enjoy this aspect, as it is a lot of fun, and can bring about significant beneficial changes, thus building self-confidence in the practitioner.

Before we get down to some serious spell casting, there are a few things you need to be aware of, to keep your magic within the spiritual doctrines of Wicca. The true Wiccan practice is more about the religion and the blending of aspects of the Universe to make life better for ourselves and the world around us than having a magic spell for every occasion.

When casting spells, remember those two words of the Wiccan Rede that carry so much meaning in them: 'Harm None.' If you wonder why I keep repeating this, it's so it will become ingrained in your soul to such an extent that you will automatically make the altruistic choice, every single time. It's important to reinforce this when we talk about magic, so you approach it in the right frame of mind and don't abuse your personal power.

Your spells should never aim to bend the will of someone else to your point of view, interfere with free will or exert control over others. If you intend to cast a spell, which will directly affect someone else, ask their permission since if you don't, your magic will not work as it should.

Spell casting relies on the right frame of mind and the preparations you make beforehand for the successful execution of your spells and enchantments. In fact, the planning and preparation are at least as important as the execution of the spell itself.

Take time to prepare yourself, both mentally and physically, before casting the spell. Assemble everything you need and be sure any ingredients or tools are exactly where you need them, so you don't need to interrupt your spell ritual to collect some herbs or a lighter for a candle. If there is a chant or special words to go with the spell, be sure to learn them before proceeding. Your focus needs to be on the energy and intent you are putting into the spell, not reading words from a paper while you try to concentrate on other aspects of the spell.

Using Magical Correspondence Tables in Spells

Check with magical correspondence tables to see if there is a particular day, or phase of the moon when the spell will work better because the energies are stronger. Correspondence tables can also help with choosing the right herbs and colors. And if you find that, for example, a spell to banish negativity requires dragon's blood incense and you don't have any, the correspondence tables will tell you it's possible to use frankincense or pine instead.

Color correspondences are also very useful to know about, especially in candle magic. Although you can always use a white candle for any spell or ritual, using the color associated with the spell you are casting will strengthen the focus of the magic. A black candle will help to banish negative energies, while a green candle is the one to use for health spells, and pink works well for attracting love. Don't worry if you don't have access to all the colors – you can tie a ribbon or cord of the appropriate color around a plain white candle, and this will help the magic along.

Correspondence tables are also useful if you are allergic to certain essential oils, or there are incense aromas you can't tolerate. It's no good getting yourself in the right frame of mind for working magic, and then finding you can't focus your energy because the smell of the jasmine incense the spell called for is making you gag. There is always an alternative – that's why correspondence tables exist.

There are lots of magical correspondence tables online for herbs, incense, essential oils, flowers, colors, and days of the week, phases of the moon, fabrics, and elements. In fact, pretty much anything you might want to use in a spell is going to have a correspondence table. To save time, keep copies of magical correspondences all together in one place, to save you hunting each time you need them. Your *Book of Shadows* is ideal for this purpose.

How Wiccan Spells Work

Wicca magic is, above all else, spiritual magic, and the highest good of all concerned should always be the priority. Cultivating this mindset will encourage the purity of thought you require for the energy to flow strongly, thus enabling your spells to work well.

Wiccans are flexible beings, and they don't feel you need to follow the instructions of any spell to the letter. On the contrary, by tailoring the spell to suit your personal requirements, your magic is stronger. You may want to alter some of the ingredients in the spell or change the wording of the chant or prayer that accompanies the ritual. This is fine, but be sure to record both the original spell and your modifications in your *Book of Shadows*.

Make notes of which spells work, which don't, and any other information that will help you to build on the success of your magic in the future. That's exactly what your *Book of Shadows* is for. Jot your notes down as you proceed, so you don't forget anything, then write the spell up later, when you have some quiet time.

Spells will never work against science and the natural world, so don't even consider casting a spell to make your hair grow two inches in a fortnight, change the color of your eyes to a fetching baby blue from their natural, nondescript brown or lose 10lbs by the end of next week. That just isn't going to happen, sweetheart! Until you have confidence in your powers to make changes and have discovered the most effective and efficient way to channel your own energy and the energy around you, don't try to run before you can walk – you are setting yourself up for major disappointments. Why not start with something basic, like the visualizations spell to build your confidence? Here a couple of really useful ones to practice with.

Parking lot spell

If you have trouble finding a convenient parking space, visualize a free space in the lot, just when you need it. Own your space and know for sure that it will be ready for you when you arrive. Visualize a car pulling out of it to make room for you. For best results, cast this spell an hour or so before you need to use the space, but if you miss that window, don't worry. Just do it as soon as you remember.

If it doesn't work the first time, try again, and make the visualization stronger and more detailed. Visualization spells have the added bonus of building your skills, so you have deeper, more meaning meditations, so something good will always come from them, even if it takes a while to get what you want.

As a side note to this, when I'm out with spiritual friends who don't know about my spell casting, I tell them I'm going to ask the Parking Angels for a space near to where I'm going. Often, this is my local crystal shop, and as it's on the coast, it's notoriously difficult to park there. I always manage to get a space right outside the shop, and my friends are amazed. So, this spell works with Angels or with Wiccan magic. It's the positive thinking that does it. You know you're going to be able to park, so of course, you are. We get back what we put out, after all.

Astral calls

Astral call spells work to bring someone you miss back into your life. Perhaps you want to reconnect with an old school friend, a previous lover, or a family member you haven't seen for a while. Astral calls will only work if the person in question really wants to move back into your circle though. Magic should never be used to persuade someone to act against their best interests, or contrary to their wishes, especially with a powerful spell like this one.

In most basic form, the spell requires you to send out an astral call for someone to contact you, and it works surprisingly well. Visualize your friend or loved one, know they are there with you, and you are both chatting as if you'll never run out of things to say to each other. Hear the laughter ringing in your ears. Soon, the person you have visualized will contact you, seemingly out of the blue. People may try to put this down to coincidence, but it's more than that. Write down the date and time you did your astral call, and it will certainly be about the same time your friend decided to contact you.

Here's a different 'Astral call' spell, with a little more to it. You need:

• A white candle anointed with sandalwood oil

• Sandalwood incense stick

• A photo of the person you want to contact

• A glass of water

• A little salt

Light the candle, then the incense. Sandalwood is good to use for wish magic like this, and for astral projection. Place the photo on your altar. Take the salt in your right hand and trickle it into the water. Make the sign of the Elemental Cross (4 equal arms) and say 'Call me' three times. Drink the water and say 'Call me' three more times. This should happen very soon

Summoning Spells

Summoning spells cover all sorts of things – basically, anything you wish to bring into your life – but by far the most asked about summoning spells are those related to love, health and money. Love spells present a bit of a dilemma for Wiccans. They don't believe in interfering with free will, and if another person is involved in the spell, they have to ask permission – which could be very embarrassing for both parties! However, there is a simply written summoning spell, which is worth a try. It goes under various names, but I call it 'Shopping for Love.'

Shopping for Love

This spell is basically a shopping list of your requirements in a lover, male or female, and you should include as much detail as possible in your 'list.' Write down the gender, body type, and height, age, and coloring, interests – whatever is important to you in a relationship should go into the spell.

Choose good quality paper that appeals to you and use a nice pen with a fine writing point. You may even want to try some calligraphy – this is no ordinary shopping list, after all! Now cast a sacred circle and sit comfortably inside it to write your spell. Use positive language in the present tense, as if the man of your dreams is already by your side.

Know this to be true – will it to be true. When you are ready, close the circle and put the spell in a safe space until it comes true. Resist the urge to re-read it – that will only weaken the magic. When your lover materializes, return the spell to Nature, by burning it, burying it or floating it on freshwater, such as a river or stream.

Red Candle Love Spell

This simple spell to summon love into your life should be cast on a Friday evening. This is the best day for love spells, as it is Venus' own day. Also, cast it during the waxing phase of the moon, as this will help build your attraction and self-confidence, which will help in bringing in your new love.

The red candle works the strongest magic because although pink is the color most associated with love, red also denotes courage and passion, both of which are required when setting out on a new relationship. Also, red is the color most associated with love in the public consciousness – think red roses for love and red hearts on Valentine's Day cards.

To cast this spell, first cast a sacred circle around a chair and small table or desk. Light the candle inside the circle and sit and gaze into its glow for a few minutes. As you do so, imagine love starting in your heart center as a warm red ball, then growing inside you until it fills your being and spills out to fill the sacred space around you. Having memorized these words beforehand repeat them 12 times as you continue to gaze into the flame of the candle:

I ask the forces of the Universe,

I ask the Spirits,

I ask the Angels overwatching me

To help this love grow stronger

This incantation is translated from an ancient language, so, unfortunately, it doesn't rhyme, which makes it more difficult to learn verbatim. However, it's a very strong yet simple spell, so it's worth persevering with it.

When you have finished, blow out the candle and put it somewhere safe until love comes into your life. Then bury it in your garden to keep your lover close.

Spells for Summoning Health

First of all, let me make it clear that medical magic – even powerful Wiccan magic – is not meant to be used instead of consulting a doctor. It's designed as a complementary treatment process to amplify the results achieved with the appropriate medical treatment.

Healing spells can be cast for spiritual, emotional and physical healing, and incorporating gentle crystal energy from clear quartz, rose quartz or amethyst will amplify the power of the spell. As with all magic, if you intend to cast a spell for someone else, ask for their permission first.

Spells for health improvement should be cast on Mondays, and again, in the waxing phase of the moon. Green is recognized as a healing color, as it is the color of the ray of Archangel Raphael, the Master Healer. With that information at the forefront of our minds, let's check out these nice straightforward healing spells.

Simple Candle Healing Spell

For this spell, you will need:

✔ Three green candles

✔ A pointed object to inscribe the candles

✔ A clear quartz crystal

Cast your sacred circle, then inscribe the name of the person you want to heal – it can be yourself too – on each candle. Arrange them in a triangular shape. There are three candles to tie in with the power of the Threefold Law – sending out three times the healing energy makes it three times more powerful.

Concentrate of the flames for a while – as long as feels right to you. Think positive, healing thoughts, then say these lines three times over as you look into the candle flames:

Healing light, healing light,

Cause this sickness to flee in flight!

It will harm no-one, including me,

As I cast this spell – so mote it be!

Once you have finished the incantation, hold the quartz crystal in your hand and meditate as the candles burn down. During the meditation, visualize whoever you are sending the healing to as happy, healthy, and full of energy.

If the person needs spiritual healing, you can substitute blue candles to symbolize emotional health. If you don't have colored candles, tie an appropriately colored ribbon or cord around a white candle.

Abracadabra Healing Spell

This must be the simplest spell ever! Quick and easy to do, and the beauty is, if you are ill yourself, it doesn't take too much concentration, so as long as you can do the necessary writing, you should soon be feeling better.

It's a very old spell, and it simply involves writing the word 'Abracadabra' on separate lines on a small piece of paper, missing off one letter each time, until you're down to a single letter 'A.' It should look something like this:

Abracadabra

Abracadabr

Abracadab

Abracada

Abracad

Abraca

Abrac

Abra

Abr

Ab

A

I've added a couple of my own adaptations to the original spell. I write the words on green paper, to symbolize Archangel Raphael, and I also write the name of the person I'm casting the spell for on the reverse. Write your disappearing words neatly, with a nice pen with a fine point. Then roll up your piece of paper and thread a cord or chain through its center.

Wear it around your neck until you – or the person you cast the spell for – are feeling better. Then bury the paper in the earth, to keep that person's energy close to you, in case you need to do the spell again. This will help amplify the magic by reinforcing the energetic connection, but you will need to start over with new paper, obviously.

Spells for Summoning Wealth

While nobody can conjure money out of thin air, and there is – unfortunately – no such thing as a money tree, there are ways in which Wiccan spells can improve your financial situation. Contrary to popular belief in some quarters, money is NOT 'The root of all evil.' It's necessary for lots of things in this day and age, and we have to find a way to make it work for us.

Money problems arise when people have a negative response to financial matters or are not sure how to plan ahead. So before attempting a wealth spell, it's a good idea to a releasing meditation to banish any negative attitudes to money or limiting beliefs. Do this release at the end of the waning moon phase in preparation for the spell. Any banishing work, whether in spells or meditation, is always more effective during the waning moon, while attraction and summoning spells work best during the waxing phase of the moon.

Saturday is a good day to cast spells to attract money, and if you want to banish debt from your life, cast your spell on a Wednesday during the waning moon phase. If you want to use a crystal for attracting money, it's citrine. Here are a couple of simple money spells you can try.

Full Moon Money Spell

The full moon marks the end of the waxing moon phase when the moon is at its fullest and most abundant. For this simple spell, you will need:

✔ A dark brown candle, but be sure the candle is not artificially colored. Brown symbolizes material possessions and financial stability.

✔ A gold-colored coin

✔ A cinnamon stick, a piece of orange peel and some dried basil. All have magical correspondences with money and increased income.

Sit in a quiet room, with just the light of the moon. Light the candle and watch the flame as you take in 30 deep breaths. As you do this, visualize yourself with lots of money, and no need to count the pennies. Place the gold coin, and the cinnamon, orange peel and basil between your palms then rub them together for a few minutes, inhaling the lovely aromas as you do so.

When you are ready, repeat this enchantment three times:

Money flow, money grow, money glow.

Now blow out the candle and put the coin in the purse or wallet you usually carry around with you.

The spell should manifest results in a few weeks, and you could also keep a small citrine crystal with the coin. I always carry citrine with my money anyway, and you might want to try this.

Set the intent to spend your money wisely and take advantage of any bargains that come your way. You will soon notice that your money seems to go further than usual, and you will be less inclined to impulse purchases.

Wiccan Abundance Spell

This is another simple yet very powerful, spell to attract abundance into your life. Even if, on paper, you are earning enough money to support yourself and your family, sometimes you find you have no time to spare for them, or when you do, you are too exhausted to enjoy it. Maybe you're spending so much time and money on childcare and travel you feel like you're just working to pay the bills and the taxes.

If you feel this way, an abundance spell can definitely help, because abundance is not just about the bottom line on your payslip – it's about a good work/life balance that works well for everyone concerned, whatever your pay scale. On the other hand, if you just want more money for more 'stuff,' this spell is not going to work, because, as with all Wiccan magic, you need to approach spell casting with honest intent to make beneficial changes, not just to grab more money because you can. As long as you approach the spell with a feeling of gratitude for what you already have, but a sincere wish to improve your life for your highest good, this powerful spell will work for you.

You will need:

✔ Some sort of copper bowl – it doesn't need to be large, but it does need to be copper for the spell to work.

✔ Three gold-colored coins

✔ Fresh spring or river water, gathered where there is flow. If this is not available,

You can buy a small bottle of spring water that has been bottled at source and not messed around with.

This spell must be cast on the night of a full moon; otherwise, it will not work for your highest good. Sit in a quiet, darkened room, and concentrate on your wish for abundance as, one by one, you throw the gold coins into the copper bowl, half-filled with spring water.

Gaze into the water until you see the moon reflected on its surface. Then focus your energy in the bowl and repeat these words three times:

I desire abundance and increased prosperity

For which I shall be grateful beyond eternity

Leave the coins in the water overnight, then dry them with a clean yellow or white piece of fabric and put them in your purse. Keep them separate from other coins, to ensure you don't spend them because this spell is for ongoing abundance.

The Kinds of Magic – Spells From Anything!

By now, you should have got the message that spell casting is all about the intent and the focus, not so much about the tools you use. They just help to make associations with the magic you create – they are not essential, and although spells are rituals, they are also personal to you. That means you don't have to follow a spell word for word, deed for deed for it to be successful. It's all about what YOU want from the spell, and what YOU put into it because you have to help the Universe to help you, rather than just sitting back and waiting for miracles to happen.

Life is the miracle; we as Wiccans just nudge it along to make sure our lives go as we deserve and desire. You can perform a spell with just your will and a mirror, and I'll prove it to you.

Charisma Spell

The Charisma Spell goes like this:

When you get out of bed in the morning, before you do anything at all – even use the bathroom - go to the nearest mirror. Examine your face, focus on your intent, and repeat these words three times, with feeling:

'I am a beautiful person. I am beautiful inside and out.'

Later, when you're applying make-up or styling your hair, repeat the exercise, then do it again before you get into your bed at night.

How long should you do this spell? For as long as it needs for the message to hit home, and to be certain, you are a beautiful person without having to talk to a mirror. You can vary the incantation if you like. Try something a bit more edgy, or more suited to your style, like:

'I'm hot to trot.'

'Glow with health and beauty.'

'I am the perfect version of me.'

'I love me, as I see myself.'

Quite frankly, what you say during this ritual is not important – it's the way you say it, and your frame of mind when you speak to yourself. Speak with sincerity, straight from the heart. Your mind is doing all the work in this lovely simple spell, making you feel increasingly better about yourself and how you appear to others. The spell works well for guys too – they also have their moments of self-doubt, and this spell can help with that.

I hope you now believe that your mind is capable of many things and that you have the power to shift your focus at will and bring magical changes into your life and the lives of others. If you are still feeling apprehensive about casting spells, or you don't believe fully in the power of your own mind and spirit, try a few simple spells with familiar ingredients to build your confidence in yourself and your Wiccan strength of faith.

Let's take a quick look at the different types of magic you can conjure up, even if you are very new to the Wiccan Way. (pun intended!)

Candle Magic

Not so long ago, candles were essential to bring light in the darkness. These days, we don't need them for that, but they do provide a gentle ambiance, whatever you are doing, whether it is related to Wicca or not.

For centuries, witches and pagans have used candles in rituals and spell casting, and there are many candle magic spells around. They are ideal for newcomers to Wicca, because candle spells are usually simple, with few ingredients, and they can help you understand the magical correspondences in spells. Candle magic often incorporates herbs, oils, and other items, all of which have magical correspondences, and you will learn these as you go along.

Here are a couple of simple candle magic spells to give you an idea of how simple, satisfying, and successful candle magic can be.

Candle Spell to Banish Negativity

You cannot be truly happy if there is negativity in your life, which is keeping your energy stuck in a bad place. This powerful yet simple spell will banish negativity and allow you to discover the happiness you deserve. You need:

✔ A black candle (For banishing negativity and protection)

✔ Sandalwood oil (For the protection and heightening psychic abilities)

✔ Dried basil, mint or white sage (All good for protection and cleansing)

Make sure the herbs are finely crushed into tiny pieces, using a pestle and mortar. Rub the oil over the candle, and roll it in the herbs, making sure as much as possible adhere to the surface. Now stand the candle in a stable holder and light it. Watch out for the odd spark from the oil and herbs, and make sure the candle is in a safe place.

While the candle burns, chant an incantation designed to banish negative energy, bad attitudes, and anything else that doesn't serve you and embrace the happiness and peace you deserve.

You can write the incantation yourself, or use a suitable one from elsewhere, but be aware that the magic will be even stronger if you use your own words, straight from the heart. Repeat this incantation three times. Now allow the candle to burn out and sit and focus on releasing the negativity to make way for the good things waiting to move into the empty space as you release everything that needs to go. If any remnants of wax are left, bury it outside, as far away from your door as possible.

Spells for happiness are dependent on banishing all negative energy so that positive energy can flow freely. For them to work, you must be ready and willing to let sadness and negativity leave your energetic space and be receptive to happiness. You also need to believe that you are worthy of happiness and embrace it.

Happiness is not easily quantified since everyone's perception is different, but negativity, which is already present, is identifiable, and because of this, it's simple to focus on and banish. Often, the ritual of banishing negativity is all you need to do in order to welcome happiness into your life.

Candle Marriage Spell

This spell is doubly useful. You can cast it to attract a new love into your life, or if you want to encourage your lover to pop the question, you can take it a stage further. You need:

✔ A simple baking tray

✔ Two tea light candles

✔ 2 Tarot cards – one for you and one for your intended. Shuffle the deck, then choose two cards, or select any 'flying' cards that fall out of the deck.

✔ Two rose quartz crystals to symbolize love.

The candles for this spell symbolize light and love. You can use plain tea lights, or colored and/or fragranced ones. Check the magical correspondences to make sure you choose colors/fragrances for love. For best results, cast a spell on Friday evening, during a waxing moon phase.

Place the baking tray in front of you, then position the tea lights in the top corners of the tray. Place one Tarot card below each candle and position a crystal on top of each card. Bless the cards and the candles by making the sign of the Pentagram over them with your hand.

Slide the cards and candles together over the tray until they are touching. Bless the ritual again for strengthened energy and reaffirm your trust in the spell.

If marriage is on your mind, place the cards one over the other, with both crystals on top, and slide one candle behind the other. In the middle of the tray, you should have two candles at the top, and two Tarot cards, laid one on top of the other, with two rose quartz crystals on them, below the candles.

There are literally hundreds – if not thousands – of candle spells around. Browse books and the Internet and try those that appeal. I work a lot with crystals, for healing and for magic, so I always bring them into candle magic to amplify the energy, but if you don't have crystals, the spells will work equally well with just the candles. It just may take a little longer to get the results you're looking for.

Herbal magic

The original 'witches' were wise women of their village who made natural remedies from herbs, and herbal magic plays an important part in modern Wiccan practice. Herbs in Wiccan terms does not just apply to the leafy stuff you can find in supermarkets or grow yourself for cooking – it covers anything in plant life that can be used in spells. Tree bark, grasses, and weeds such as dandelion are likely to appear in herbal magical correspondence tables and spell recipes.

People who work mainly with herbal magic are known as kitchen witches, and there is a special Wicca tradition for them. They are mostly solo practitioners and can cast spells, make potions and teas and even cook cakes and biscuits which are surprisingly powerful in bringing about beneficial change. If you grow your own herbs, your magic will be even stronger, as right from the seed stage, you will be nurturing your plants and thinking of how to use them to best advantage once they mature.

People who talk to plants are no longer regarded as strange – science has proved that plants - just like people and animals – respond well to kindness and care. Be kind to your herbs, and they will reward you by working with you to create fabulous herbal magic.

Herb Wreaths to Attract Love, Money, and Wellbeing

A good way to keep herb magic close is to make a wreath to hang on your door, and this also the best way to learn about herb correspondences. All you need is a wreath frame from a craft supplies shop, some florist wire, and colored ribbon, depending on what the wreath is for.

For example, if you want to attract love into your life, make a wreath with a mix of lavender, peppermint, apple blossom, marjoram, basil, and other herbs suitable for love. Decorate your wreath with a pretty pink ribbon.

A prosperity wreath could include bay leaves, chamomile, basil, clover, and applewood. Finish it off with a gold ribbon to attract abundance.

For healing and general wellbeing, choose lavender, rosemary, apple blossom, feverfew, and olive. Dress it with a bright green ribbon, the color of the healing ray of Archangel Raphael.

Start your herb magic journey by learning the magical correspondences of just a few herbs and see how you get on with simple spells before expanding your repertoire of herbal magic. Here's a couple of simple herb spells to get you started. You can find many more in books and online.

Herb Spell to Open Your Heart to Love

This simple spell involves mixing herbs and flower petals together in a small drawstring bag made of natural fabric like silk or cotton. Carry the pouch with you to help release any unacknowledged energy blocks that may be closing you off from love. This spell is most effective when performed on a Friday during the waning moon phase, as you are casting the spell to banish negative energies that are preventing you from finding the love you so richly deserve. You need:

✔ Six cloves

✔ One teaspoon mugwort, dried

✔ One teaspoon lemon balm

✔ One teaspoon St John's wort

✔ One tablespoon rose petals, dried

✔ ¼ cup chamomile flowers

✔ Small bowl

✔ One pink candle

Light the candle, and meditate on it for a minute or two, until your mind is calm, clear, and focused on your intent. Mix the herbs together in the bowl with your fingers, then add the herbs and flowers to the drawstring bag and tie it off tightly so nothing can leak out.

Hold the sachet in your right hand, as you are giving your energy blocks to the Universe to transmute to positive energy, which can then be used by someone who needs it. (As an aside, if you wonder why the God and athame or wand are traditionally placed to the left of a Wiccan altar, and the Goddess, chalice, and bowl to the right, it's all tied to giving and receiving. This is valid for many things in Wicca. If you are meditating with a crystal, you will hold it in your left hand, to receive its energies. However, if you are doing healing using a crystal or a healing wand, you will hold it in your right hand, since Spirit is sending the healing through you as a gift to the recipient, so you use the right hand.)

Back to the spell – as you hold the sachet of herbs in your hand, close your eyes and visualize a white light starting at your heart center then expanding to fill your entire being. After a few moments, see a pink light start from the same place, and grow to merge with the white light. Say this verse – or something similar you have written yourself – three times:

As below, so above,

I relinquish all invisible barriers to love.

As above, so below,

My healed heart welcomes love to flow.

If you wish, you can hold a rose quartz crystal in your left hand to amplify the energy. Let the candle burn away as you sit quietly and visualize your energy blocks, leaving your space, allowing you to open your heart to love again.

Carry the sachet until you feel your energy shifting positively and keep it near your bed or under your pillow at night. Once you feel you no longer need to hold onto the sachet, return the herbs to the Earth for purification. Either bury them or scatter them on grass or soil outside the perimeter of your home.

Basil and Garlic Prosperity Spell

This simple spell will attract more money for those of us who have too much month left at the end of our salary! If you can get a wooden box for this, it's better, but if not, you can use something like a shoebox instead. You will need:

✔ Five fresh basil leaves

✔ One head of garlic

✔ Essential oil for prosperity, such as cinnamon, sandalwood, patchouli

✔ A fairly high denomination note in your local currency – the higher the value, the stronger the magic.

✔ A white cotton handkerchief, or a square of white cloth. A paper hankie will NOT do.

✔ Wooden box or shoebox, large enough for your paper money to lie flat on the bottom of the box.

Place the money in the bottom of the box and put the garlic head on top of it. Say this verse or something similar you have written yourself, three times:

'Tis time, 'tis time,

I connect and combine

Timeless magic with fresh allure

May my funds increase and stay secure

Now spread the basil leaves around the garlic head, and cover everything with the handkerchief. Close the box and keep it under your bed until your finances improve.

One thing to remember about herb magic is that you need to build a relationship with the herbs you use. Respect them for their properties, handle them with care, and keep growing plants well-watered and in the right place to flourish.

Crystal Magic

Before we leave spells behind for now, we'll take a look at a form of magic that is very dear to me – crystal magic. I love working with crystals because their energy is so powerful it's palpable. Just holding the right crystal to match your mood is soothing and comforting, or energizing and uplifting, whatever you may need at a particular moment in time. Crystals love to help us with healing, protection, magic, and self-care, and they are beautiful to look at as a bonus.

The energy in crystals interacts with peripheral energies, including our thoughts, and that's what makes them such powerful allies in Wiccan practice. If you're new to crystals and are concerned about choosing the 'right' crystals, don't worry – they will find you, or you will be drawn to them. There is no such thing as a bad energy crystal, although some crystal energies will clash with your energetic field, so if you get a bad vibe from certain crystals, give them a miss, however much you like them.

Crystals can be used in spells in their own right, or as an amplifier to the energy in other spells. I almost always include a suitable crystal to give spells a bit more oomph – I'll use rose quartz in love spells, black tourmaline for protection spells and citrine for prosperity and abundance spells.

Placing a clear quartz crystal with tarot and oracle cards, healing books or the *Book of Shadows* will amplify the energy, improve communication, and strengthen psychic connections. I keep all my card decks on the bottom shelf of my crystal display cupboard, and since I started doing that, my readings have become more accurate and insightful. That means I can give my sitters so much more information and guidance.

When you work with crystals, program them with your intent, and don't use the same rose quartz for healing and spells – have a different crystal for each job you want to work with them on, otherwise the focus will be watered down and the magic won't work well, if it works at all.

Here are a couple of simple crystal magic spells to get you started. As we've mentioned before, check on the magical correspondence tables to be sure you have the right crystal for the spell you wish to cast.

Crystal Communication Spell

Blue crystals are generally used for improving communication and are associated with the throat chakra. This spell will help you conduct more effective conversations, remaining calm amid the drama, and speaking out clearly and confidently. You need:

✔ I lapis lazuli or sodalite crystal, small enough to carry around with you.

✔ A clear quartz and an amethyst crystal. Amethyst is for calmness, and clear quartz amplifies the energy of the other crystals.

✔ A white candle

Sit quietly at your altar, or a table. Place the amethyst and clear quartz in front of the candle, then light it and gaze into the flame to clear your mind. Hold the lapis lazuli or sodalite in your left hand, close your eyes, and say this affirmation, or something similar, three times:

I communicate effectively on all levels as I speak my truth

Now close your eyes, take a few deep breaths, and visualize yourself feeling relieved and empowered because a conversation has gone exactly as you wanted it to. You don't need to play a conversation, real or imagined, in your head, but really feel that relief, and allow the positive vibes to flow from your heart center, down your arm, and into the bluestone. It will feel warmer in your hand, and you may feel the energy in your hand chakra as a tingling sensation.

Sit like this until your intuition tells you the stone is charged with your intent, allowing the candle to burn down

Black Tourmaline Protection Spell

Black stones are great for grounding and protection for people and property. A friend was having problems with her neighbors, so I performed this ritual, and a week later, the problem was solved when the person causing the problem went away after breaking up with her partner. She came back a few weeks later and was completely different. That was a year ago now, and relations are still calm and settled. For this spell, you will need:

✔ I black tourmaline wand, about 6 – 10 inches long

✔ Another black tourmaline stone

✔ A white sage incense stick

Start by cleansing the whole house, inside and out, by walking the property with a smoking white sage incense stick. Have as many doors and windows open as is practical, to allow the free flow of all energies, good and bad. As you move around, focus your intent on clearing the property of any residual negative energy. Visualize a pink aura of unconditional love drifting around the house and through it.

Return indoors, and if the white sage is still smoldering, place it in an incense holder for safety, then close the doors and windows. Take the two pieces of tourmaline and place one just inside the front door – or the door, which is normally opened to admit visitors and tradespeople to the house. Make sure nobody can trip over it, but it needs to be in a place where everyone who enters must walk past it.

Now stand facing the closed front door, hold the tourmaline wand in both hands, and rest it against the door at shoulder height, as you repeat this three times:

May all who enter through this door

Be kind in thought forevermore

Hate and spite we will never see

In this home, so mote it be

Now place the tourmaline wand next to a party wall, if the property is semi-detached. Otherwise, place it against the nearest wall to the neighboring property. This should bring harmony to the household and keep away negative energies from people and the spirit world.

Put the tourmaline in the light of a full moon if you have a lot of visitors, or if you feel the energy in your home shifting negatively. This will cleanse and recharge the crystal with moon energy. You will need to repeat the spell again each time the crystals are moved for cleansing and charging, but it's very quick and easy to recast.

You should now have enough information to cast your first Wiccan spell. Remember, your intention and energy should be positive when working magic, and keep in mind the Wiccan Rede exhortation to 'Harm None,' otherwise, your spells could miss the mark, and may even cause problems rather than solving them. In the next chapter, we'll look at divination techniques and hexes and curses. Blessed Be!

Chapter 8: Divination, Hexes, and Curses

Divination is a form of magic that has been used for centuries, by wise women, magicians, and psychics. It differs from Wiccan magic in two respects. Divination is not exclusive to Wicca or witchcraft. It can be practiced by just about anyone and is often used by mediums and psychics.

The second-way divination differs from other forms of magic is that it does not attempt to make changes in personal or external circumstances and/or situations. Rather, divination is a method of foretelling the future by various means, including, but not limited to, crystal balls, palm reading, pendulum dowsing, tarot and oracle cards, and psychometry – the skill of reading the energies in personal objects.

Divination can also be used to uncover the knowledge that needs to be revealed in order to give guidance and encouragement to sitters. That's the term for people who visit psychics for information to help them make decisions or solve dilemmas. Let's take a brief look at how divination methods can be used to help in

Wiccan practice, both for ourselves and to help others.

Tarot and Oracle Cards

People have been reading and interpreting cards ever since cards came into existence. The most well-known divination cards are tarot and oracle cards, but anyone who is skilled at card reading can give a pretty accurate reading from a pack of ordinary playing cards. Like all magic and spiritual work, the real skill is in interpreting the energy of the cards; decks of cards, whether tarot or oracle, are simply tools to aid in the interpretation and strengthen the link with Spirit so that the sitter can receive as much information as possible.

When you are new to Wicca and spirituality, it can be a bit intimidating when faced with the huge array of different decks available. The traditional Tarot consists of 78 cards, 22 Major Arcana, and 56 Minor Arcana, and each card has its own special meanings, as well as the extra intuitive items that come through to the reader. And depending on which deck you choose, the artist will have added their own intuitive details, since the very act of designing cards for divination is channeled from Spirit.

However, once you have an idea of the basic principles of card reading, you will soon be reading with the best of them. Just place your trust in your own abilities, and your connection with the Universe, and practice, practice, practice as often as you can.

I was very wary of reading cards, until a couple of years ago, when I joined a small psychic circle. The leader was an excellent card reader, who preferred to read for sitters from cards rather than read mediumistically, although we regularly did both at the circle. Her enthusiasm and knowledge rubbed off on me, and with her encouragement, I have reached the stage where I am confident doing public oracle card readings, although it will be a while yet before I know enough to read the Tarot, other than in practice at the circle.

A couple of weeks ago, I did mini readings for flood victims in our local area, and of the 20 sitters, I only knew two people personally, and not all that well at that. However, I was thrilled to hit the spot with everything I said.

I'm not telling you this to blow my own trumpet. I realize that I am only able to do this because Spirit give me their love, confidence, and support, as well as helpful information for my sitters. I'm sharing this convince you that, even if you are terrified by Tarot or overwhelmed by oracle cards, as I was not so very long ago if you have faith in yourself, your guides and the

Universe, you can do anything you set your heart on. You are the manufacturer of miracles – remember that!

The Difference between the Tarot and Oracle Cards

The principal difference between the two types of the deck is that oracle cards can be based on anything of spiritual significance, and there can be any number in the deck. There are some parameters for the design of Tarot decks. There must be 78 cards in total, as mentioned previously. The characters for each card must also be the same, although the depictions can vary. Also, there are four suits in the Minor Arcana, as with regular playing cards, although there are 14 in each suit, compared to 13 in playing cards.

Traditionally, the four suits of the Tarot are Wands, Cups, Swords, and Pentacles. They correspond, in order, to the Elements of Fire, Water, Air, and Earth. There are a number of other correspondences in various areas of life and Nature, and you really need a basic understanding of these correspondences, but rather than overload you with too much information and lots of text, here's a handy

Tarot table with each of the correspondences listed:

Correspondence	Wands	Cups	Swords	Pentacles
Other Names	Rods, Staves	Chalices, Goblets	Blades, Athames	Discs, Coins
*Elements	Fire	Water	Air	Earth
Colors	Yellow	Red	Indigo	Green
Seasons	Spring	Summer	Winter	Fall
Symbolism	Creativity Action, Passion	Love Emotion Empathy	Thought Challenge Observation	Health Wealth The Body
Zodiac Signs	Aries Leo Saggitarius	Cancer Scorpio Pisces	Gemini Libra Aquarius	Taurus Virgo Capricorn
Realm	Spirit	Heart	Mind	Home
Playing Cards	Clubs	Hearts	Spades	Diamonds
Gender	Male	Female	Male	Female
Direction	South	West	North	East

• In some Tarot decks, such as The Good Tarot by Colette Baron-Reid, the suits are named after the Elements they correspond with

Tarot is such a huge subject, I will just leave you with this taster, as there is still a lot to cover. There are many online and 'real-time' workshops and courses for learning the Tarot if you wish to further your knowledge.

Unlike the Tarot, oracle cards do not have fixed themes. Typically, there are anywhere between 44 and 60 cards, or maybe more, depending on the designer of the deck and their purpose. They can represent angels, dragons, butterflies, birds, animals, sea creatures, Nature – you name it, and there is probably an oracle deck designed around it! Oracle cards are more for giving guidance in the now and answering questions. There is not so much emphasis on the future and incoming stuff.

Divination with Pendulums

Although there are many beautiful pendulums around, you can make your own as long as you have a weight and a chain or cord. Last week, I worked some great divination magic with a friend's crystal pendant and told complete strangers what they needed to know. Pendulum dowsing is a simple way to check on facts or clarify messages.

Choose a pendulum whose energy draws you, or which you are drawn to. Cleanse it, and program into it your intent to work with your pendulum for the highest good for all concerned.

Before doing any work with Spirit – for it is Spirit who works with the pendulum energy – be sure to protect yourself psychically, either with a spell or a short visualization. You are now ready to work with your pendulum.

Hold the pendulum steady and ask it to show you a 'Yes' and a 'No.' There is no conventional answer, but the combined energies of yourself and your pendulum will move the crystal in a straight line or a circle. Before using the pendulum each time, ask this question three times over:

Are you working in the love and light of Divine Spirit?

If you do not get three 'yes' answers, you may need to do more cleansing and programming on your pendulum. If you feel any negative energy around it, bury it outside and do a banishing ritual. Your pendulum should be a spiritual tool, not a means of psychic attack.

When working with a pendulum, the questions need to be worded in the right way, or you will get a confusing answer. They can be very useful for finding lost objects – work around the room and ask if you are getting close. The results can be spectacular,

It takes time to build up a working relationship with your pendulum, so don't be discouraged if you don't 'get' it straight away. Look for a good book, or try YouTube for further information.

As previously mentioned, there are numerous methods of divination, but the ones I've just mentioned are the most popular, and the most easily grasped for beginners. As with all things Wicca, practice makes perfect – well, almost! Above all, have fun, trust your guides, and be open to experience and learning.

Hexes and Curses

No self-respecting adherent to the Ways of Wicca will ever place a hex or a curse on anyone, as Wiccan magic is geared for good, and negative magic goes against the Wiccan Rede instruction to 'Harm none.' Also, consider the

Threefold Law, which states that all deeds, good or bad, are returned in triplicate.

If you are concerned that you may be the target of a magical attack, stay calm, and think it through. If someone tells you they've cursed you, it's probably nonsense, because hexes and curses are, like most magic, performed privately and kept secret.

Divination with a pendulum or crystal ball can find out if there really is a bad spell on you, or if you're just having a run of bad luck. That does happen, even to Wiccans! Ask a trusted friend to do this, since your own concerns over outcome may adversely affect the energy, and you will get a false answer.

The best protection against negative magic is defense, so carry a piece of protective crystal such as black tourmaline, obsidian, or hematite. You may also want to put a protective circle around yourself or cast a protection spell. If despite this, the magic makes it through, there are lots of protection spells in books and online.

If your intentions are good, the Universe will protect you – believe that, and trust in the power of light over dark. Before our tour of the Ways of Wicca comes to an end, let's examine the one element of Wiccan practice around pretty much everything else revolves – The Wiccan Wheel of the Year. Blessed Be!□

Chapter 9: The Wiccan Wheel of the Year, Sabbats and Esbats

While the idea of a natural circle of life for all living things has been around since pre-Christian times, the Wiccan Wheel of the Year is a fairly modern concept that only was termed as such in the 1960s.

In essence, the Wheel of the Year is the Wicca calendar of faith, and a way to honor the 8 pagan Sabbats of the year. These celebrations can trace their origins back to ancient rituals drawn from harvests, solar festivals and fire rituals from northern Europe, including derivations from Roman, Greek, Celtic and Germanic tribes and cultures.

Each of these occasions is celebrated in varying degrees by pagans all over the world, but Wicca is the only religion known to celebrate all eight sabbats. No other religion in the world does this, but celebrating the Wheel of the Year can be celebrated by people of any religion or none. In these eco-friendlier times, more and more people are connecting with Nature and the Earth, or Mother Gaia as many people term it, and observance of and reverence of the miracles of life is becoming more widespread.

At the very core of the Wiccan religion is the strong connection between Nature, the Universe, the Divine, and daily life, and the Wheel of the Year honors this. The eight Sabbats are basically Wicca seasons, and some are more meaningful than others, but they are all celebrated with Wiccan enthusiasm and joy.

In brief, the four Greater Sabbats are when Universal energy is at its zenith, so they are very important dates in the Wicca calendar – a bit like Christmas and Easter for Christians, but without the insane commercialism. The four Lesser Sabbats celebrate the equinoxes and solstices that mark the familiar changing seasons of the year. However, thanks to climate change and other considerations, the shifts between the seasons appear less noticeable with each passing year.

Wicca has a number of links with Anglo-Saxon and Celtic culture and symbolism, which is echoed in the names given to the various festivals celebrated during the Wheel of the Year. Many of the names referred to by English speakers owe their origins to Celtic and Germanic etymology.

These are the Wiccan sabbats, listed in the order in which they are celebrated. Like the signs of the Zodiac, the first sabbat does not coincide with the beginning of the calendar year:

Samhain - 31 October

Samhain is the first chronologically, and also the holiest of the Greater Sabbats, which in many Wicca traditions marks their New Year. The name is Gaelic in origin and means 'Summer's end.' It celebrates the last of the trio of Wiccan harvests that commence with Lammas. Samhain is one of only two days in the Wiccan year in which the veil that divides living souls from the world of spirit is at its most permeable, and the connection with Spirit is amplified.

At Samhain, the dead are honored with candles and prayers. This has parallels with the way Latin cultures commemorate the Day of the Dead – or Dia de Los Muertos - on 1 November. To Wiccans though, Samhain means so much more than simply remembering those who have passed to Spirit. Communication with Spirit is more easily achieved now, so Wiccans will ask for support, guidance, and advice from the higher powers. Magic is at its most powerful at Samhain.

Preparations now begin in earnest for the arrival of winter. Seeds are collected and dried, ready to be planted in the spring, and so the cycle of Life and Nature continues. This is mirrored in the stages of being of the Goddess and the God. At Samhain, the waning God reaches the Underworld, while the Goddess joyfully receives the seed for the new, reborn God, celebrating the cycle of life and death, birth and rebirth.

Yule 21 – 23 December

Alternatively known as the Midwinter Solstice, Yule is the first of the Lesser Sabbats to be celebrated during the Wiccan Wheel of the Year.

If you really want to rattle a Wiccan's cage, try calling Yule 'The pagan alternative to Christmas.' Yule pre-dates Christianity by a long time, with some experts believing the first Yule was celebrated in Neolithic times. That's between 12,000 and 3,500 BC, which, even at the late end of the Neolithic Age, was around 3,500 years before the birth of Jesus.

Christmas is actually a Catholic construct since nobody can know with any certainty when Jesus was born. Estimates range from September to February, but many theology experts believe that Christmas, like some other Christian festivals, was placed around the time of Yule to draw attention away from pagan celebrations and focus more on God.

Another, rather less scholarly, opinion is that the early Christians envied good times the pagans were having and wanted to join the party. Whatever your belief – and either explanation could easily tally with the date choice – bear in mind that Yule and Christmas are absolutely different, in sentiment and celebration.

Yule coincides with the beginning of winter – the days are now shorter, but from Yule onwards, the nights get shorter. Some Wiccan traditions celebrate Yule as their New Year rather than Samhain, but the New Year aspect of both festivals is a secondary consideration since the Wheel of the Year is about Nature, not chronology, so to Wiccans, the calendar aspect of the year is secondary to the natural turning of the seasons.

Yule is the time to celebrate family life and to be grateful for good friends. Small gifts are exchanged, accompanied by much feasting and celebration. It's also the time when the Yule Log is lit to mark the rebirth of the God, and the coming of new light into the world. Yule shares these elements with the Christian Christmas, but there are also many differences in the two festivals.

Imbolc - 2 February

If you are not familiar with the name of this sabbat, you might recognize it from one of the alternative names for Imbolc – Candlemas. This is the name given to the Christian celebration of both Jesus' first entry into the temple and the purification of Mary. It's another Catholic creation. Like Christmas, it's probably celebrated on this day as a diametric opposite of the pagan celebration, since again, nobody can state these dates with any authority after more than 2000 years.

Imbolc – which can also be referred to as the Festival of Lights – is the second Greater Sabbat of the Wheel of the Year, and this holiday is all about new beginnings and purification. Spring is just around the corner, so it's an appropriate time for initiations into the Wiccan Way, and thorough cleansing.

Wiccans spring clean just like the rest of us, but the Imbolc clean encompasses the spiritual as well as the physical. Anything that is no longer relevant or practical is released physically and emotionally at this time, and blessings are called down on the house its occupants, whether they have two legs or four.

At Imbolc, candles are lit at sundown and will burn until sunrise, symbolically illuminating the path for spring. It's a time to clear physical and emotional space for new ideas and practices by purging things that no longer serve us through the cleansing power of fire. In Wicca, there is no sin – nothing is considered wrong as long as it 'Harms none,' and that directive includes the self. Imbolc is, above all else, a time of spiritual cleansing, so it is significant across all traditions of Wicca.

Ostara 21 – 23 March

Also identified as the Spring or Vernal Equinox, Ostara is the second of the Lesser Sabbats. Now, the days and nights are equally divided across 24 hours, so Ostara marks the true beginning of Spring. It's time to plant seeds for new growth, so the seeds collected at Samhain are returned to Mother Gaia as both spiritual and physical offerings, to maintain the natural cycle of life.

Ostara is often symbolized by eggs to celebrate fertility and the birth of new life, but once more, the focus of Ostara is very different to the Christian Easter. In Wicca, the egg represents the Goddess and the God. The yolk stands for the dynamic energy of the adolescent God. The white marks the nurturing power of the Goddess, who is now in her Maiden form, and the shell is symbolic of the union of the male and female aspects as a whole.

At Ostara, it's time for spiritual growth as well as growth in Nature. Creativity and renewal of spirit are paramount, and new projects, whether spiritual or physical, are blessed at this time.

Beltane – 1 May

For centuries, long before Wicca became a recognized religion, May Day has been celebrated in many cultures, right across the spectrum of pagan, secular and Christian traditions. A world-famous May Day commemoration takes place each year in Padstow, on the beautiful, rugged north coast of Cornwall in England. On 'Obby Oss Day,' as it is locally known, up to 30,000 people from all over the world will squeeze themselves into the sleepy fishing village. The maypole dancing enjoyed by adults and children alike in Padstow is a central component of Beltane celebrations. Maypoles are emblematic of fertility.

Beltane is the third Greater Sabbat, and it's the second time in the Wheel of the Year when the veil between the living and the dead is at its thinnest point. Once more, the dead are commemorated, magic spells are cast, and procreation is at the forefront, as the seeds planted at Ostara start to grow.

It's a time for mating to take place in Nature across the species, and for Wiccan hand-fasting ceremonies. These are similar to Christian marriages, and indeed May ushers in the marriage season. The Goddess and the God are more mature, and just like other beings of energy, they embrace the sensuality of the season by consummating their union, thus becoming united in all senses of the word.

Beltane is when Wiccan craft fairs commence, as creativity is highlighted now. For Wiccans, it's an exciting time of year, full of opportunities for abundance and spiritual growth.

Litha – 21 – 23 June

Also known as the Summer Solstice, Litha ushers in the summer, when the days are as long as they can be. The word 'solstice' comes from the Latin meaning 'when the sun stands still,' and at Litha, the sun is at its zenith in the sky. It's the third of the Lesser Sabbats, a time to celebrate fulfillment and fruition. Litha is the acknowledgment that everything in the Universe is coming together, both physically and spiritually.

Nighttime feasts make the most of the longer days, and Mother Gaia's bounty is shared. All too soon, the seeds of the fruits will be returned to the Earth to start the cycle of life again. The Goddess and the God assume their rightful places as Lord and Lady of Wicca, and from now on, the nights begin to close in, and the power and strength of the God start to wane, along with the daylight.

Lammas – 1 August

Lammas, also known as Lughnasadh, is the last of the Greater Sabbats, and it signals the approaching end of summer. This is the first of the three harvests in the Wheel of the Year, the last being Samhain, and it's a time to reflect, review, and learn from past mistakes.

If you are wondering about the two names, Lughnasadh came first. It's a Celtic/Gaelic celebration of the gods of the sun and the grain. Lammas, meaning 'loaf mass,' dates from the early Christian practice of taking the loaves made from the grain harvest to church to be blessed. Remember that back then, they couldn't just pop to the shops for a loaf of bread – if the grain harvest failed, they didn't eat, so it was a natural thing to want to give thanks for a successful harvest.

Lammas is termed the grain harvest since it coincides with the first harvest of ripe grain, and it's an important harvest because the grain will feed everyone through the winter. The God uses the last of his energies for this harvest, so he now starts the descent to the Underworld.

Mabon – 21 – 23 September

Mabon is the Autumn Equinox, and also the final Lesser Sabbat of the Wheel of the Year. This is the 'Witches' Thanksgiving,' which bears similarities to the Christian Harvest Festival

Mabon is a time for quiet reflection as you make preparations for winter. The God continues his descent to the Underworld, which will culminate at Samhain. And so the Wiccan Wheel of the Year continues to turn.

Esbats

While the Wheel of the Year is built around the sun and the progression of the Goddess and the God, esbats are celebrations of the full moon. They are totally concerned with the Goddess and are about getting together to celebrate, make magic, and develop the connection with the Goddess and with Spirit. Esbats are Wiccan party times, and they are celebrated by both covens and solitary practitioners.

There, then, is a basic grounding in the Wheel of the Year, Sabbats and Esbats. As with all things

Wicca, there is so much to learn, it can't possibly be covered in detail, and in any case, a book for beginners is not the place to do so. I hope you've enjoyed your introduction to the Ways of Wicca, and that, like so many of us, you will grow and flourish, spiritually and mentally, in the Wiccan way. Blessed Be!

Conclusion

In this book, I have covered the basics you need to learn about the Ways of Wicca and grow spiritually in the faith. There is a vast amount to learn, and a book like this can only hope to scratch the surface. That said, the Wiccan Way is about study and knowledge for self-growth, so it serves no purpose to be spoon-fed Wiccan practice.

As we have seen, there is nothing scary or special about Wicca – it's based on working with energy and with the Universe to make ourselves the best version of us possible, and to respect and care for the Universe in preparation for those who follow us to Earth.

Wicca is a way of life, so it's a major commitment, but it can be very rewarding, and you can learn so much about yourselves, Nature, the Universe and your fellow beings here on Planet Earth. I wish you good fortune and abundance, as you journey along the Ways of Wicca. Blessed Be!

Glossary of Terms Used in Wicca

Here's a useful explanation of the main terms used in Wiccan belief and practice. Refer to this whenever you come across a term you don't understand.

Altar: Any flat surface, indoors or outdoors, where you assemble a collection of objects to assist you when meditating or performing rituals.

Amulet: Any item or charm that is worn for protection against negative energy.

Astral Projection: Separating the spirit from the body and traveling through space. This often happens in dreams and meditations.

Athame: A short bladed ceremonial dagger used to direct energy during rituals.

Autumn Equinox: A time towards the end of September when day and night are of equal length.

Beltane: A major Wiccan festival midway between Spring Equinox and Summer Solstice, heralding the beginning of summer. It can be celebrated on 30 April or 1 May.

Blessed Be: Traditional Wiccan salutation, used as both 'hello' and 'goodbye.' May be used as a 'code' to identify oneself as Wiccan to others.

Book of Shadows: This is both a record of your own Wiccan journey and a place to list spells, charms, ritual practices, and anything else pertinent to your craft. It's a sacred text, which can be handed down through generations or to your protégés, so construct it with care and love.

Candle Magic/k: This is the use of candles of various sizes and colors to assist in spell casting and rituals.

Casting a Circle: The process of creating a cleansed, sacred space in which to perform rituals and spells.

Centering: The focus of thoughts and energies on rituals and spells.

Chakra: The term used for various energy points throughout the body. There are seven main chakras.

Chalice: A ceremonial goblet used in various rituals and spells.

Channeling: Blending with Spirit so they can bring messages and guidance through a human portal.

Chanting: Using repeated words and/or phrases, with or without music, to induce a state of trance.

Charging: Filling an object such as a crystal, wand or ceremonial chalice or dagger with energy so that spells or rituals may be more powerful. Can be achieved by placing the objects under the light of a full moon, or by the practitioner setting the intended purpose of the object.

Charm: Any object that has been charged with energy to bring good luck or protection to the carrier.

Circle: A group of like-minded people brought together for healing, discussion, or to carry out rituals.

Cleansing: The banishing of negativity from and object or person. May also be referred to as Clearing.

Coven: A gathering of Wiccans (or witches). Covens usually number 13 and can include males and females.

Crone: The third stage of evolution of the Triple Goddess. It also means a wise woman or a post-menopausal lady. Corresponds to the waning phase of the moon. Gained negative associations because of the witch hunts of medieval times.

Deity: A general term for any god or goddess.

Deosil: Moving clockwise, or in the direction of the sun. The term derives from a Gaelic word meaning 'right,' and is the opposite of 'widdershins.' Moving deosil is to travel in a safe and lucky direction.

Divination: The use of observation of signs and patterns in tarot cards, smoke, clouds, and other objects to offer insights and guidance pertinent to the situation of the questioner.

Dowsing: The use of rods or pendulums to discover water and lost items or to receive 'yes' or 'no' answers to specific questions.

Drawing Down the Moon: A ritual at the heart of the Wiccan practice, it is performed at Full Moon to draw energy from the Goddess into the Wiccan female witch to amplify their powers.

Drawing Down the Sun: A similar ritual in which a male Wiccan witch draws down the energy of the God from the sun.

Earth Magic/k: Magic that resides within the power of Mother Earth.

Earth Power: Everything is energy, which can be harnessed to create magic or cast spells. Wiccans use the natural energy of the Earth – in plants, rocks, wind, and other earthly things – when performing rituals or casting spells.

Elementals: The spirits associated with the four main elements of Earth, Air, Fire, and Water. Gnomes represent Earth, sylphs Air, salamanders Fire, and undines Water.

Elements: The Universe is composed of the four elements of Earth, Air, Fire, and Water. A fifth element – Spirit – often figures in spiritual practice.

Esbat: A Wiccan get together held at the time of the Full Moon. There may be initiations into the coven or other ceremonies, as well as healing magic. It's a time of celebration and enjoyment for everyone.

Evocation: The summoning of spirits or other non-human entities.

God: The male element of The One. This is the Horned God, or the god of the hunt. He is often, but not always, referred to as Cernunnos, and is linked to the Earth.

Goddess: The divine feminine aspect of The One is the Triple Goddess. Associated with the moon, she is seen as Maiden, Mother, and Crone.

Handfasting: Wiccan wedding ceremony.

High Priest/ess: The witch who leads the coven.

Imbolc: One of the eight sabbats of the Wiccan year. It is celebrated on 2 February and may be more familiar as Candlemas to many people. Imbolc celebrates the arrival of spring.

Invocation: A request to a goddess or other higher power for assistance, guidance, and support. A form of prayer, commonly used by Wiccans and spiritualists.

Lughnasadh: A sabbat celebrated on 1 August to mark the first harvest of the year.

Mabon: A sabbat on 21 September, celebrating the second harvest, and preparing for winter.

Magic/k: Magick – with the 'k' – is a term originally coined by the prominent 20th-century witch and occultist Aleister Crowley. It refers to spells or rituals conducted to bring about beneficial changes in people and in the environment. Unlike 'magic' – which is often more spectacular in its execution – 'magick' must not work against the laws of science and nature, or seek to bend a person's will to that of another.

Maiden: The first aspect of the Triple Goddess. A young, beautiful woman, corresponding to the waxing phase of the moon.

Mother: The nurturing aspect of the Triple Goddess, celebrating fertility and growth. She corresponds to the full phase of the moon.

Merry Meet: A traditional greeting; the Wiccan version of 'hello.'

Midsummer: The time of the summer solstice, within a day or two of 21 June. This is when the sun is at the zenith of its power.

New Moon: The first and dark phase of the moon.

Old Religion: A traditional term for witchcraft, which also includes Wicca.

The One: The Wiccan doctrine that deities are not separate from the Universe, but form part of the whole divine aspect of all that is – 'The One.'

Referring to the Goddess and the God is a personification of their aspect of 'The One.'

Ostara: Wiccan sabbat celebrated on 21 March to celebrate the coming of spring.

Pentacle: An object used in spells and rituals bearing a carving, painting or drawing of a Pentagram (defined below).

Pentagram: A five-pointed star often used as a Wiccan symbol.

Path: An individual spiritual journey.

Quarters: The compass points of north, south, east, and west, used to mark the stations in a ritual circle.

Reincarnation: The Wiccan doctrine of reincarnation varies from other beliefs. After death, souls go to Summerland – a spiritual holding place where they can contemplate their earthly lives and decide where and when they would like to be reborn into a human body again.

Ritual: A ceremony using objects, movements, and maybe incantations to bring about a change in circumstances or situations.

Runes: Basic figures constructed from short lines carved on rocks and in clay or other materials Similar to simple hieroglyphics, they are believed to contain energies that can amplify magick and the effects of spell casting.

Sabbat: A Wiccan festival of celebration aligned with nature. There are eight sabbats in the Wiccan year.

Samhain: The sabbat celebrated on 31 October, Samhain is the Wiccan equivalent of Hallowe'en.

Scry: To stare intently into an object such as a crystal ball in the expectation of seeing helpful visions.

Skyclad: The Wiccan term for nudity. Some Wiccan traditions insist on nudity during rituals, but this isn't compulsory across Wicca.

Spell: A practice conducted to bring about beneficial change.

Solitary Practitioner: A Wiccan witch who practices alone and does not belong to a coven.

Summerland: A healing, peaceful place where spirits go for reflection before returning to Earth in another incarnation.

Talisman: An object programmed to attract specific, beneficial energies to the carrier of the talisman.

The Threefold Law: The good you perform will be returned to you in triplicate during your current incarnation, as will your bad deeds. This law encourages Wiccans always to do good rather than harm.

Traditions: The variations of Wiccan practice which have a common thread running through, but differ in some ways. There are a number of traditions to choose from, although some may have stringent entry conditions.

Underworld: The final destination of the souls of the dead after their various reincarnations. It is the province of the Horned God.

Wicca: A recognized religion derived from Celtic pagan tradition. Modern Wicca is the brainchild of Gerald Gardner, a retired civil servant from the UK who unveiled his new religion in the mid-1950s when the last of the laws against witchcraft were repealed.

Wiccan Rede: A sacred text, the main message of which is, 'An' ye harm none, do as ye will.' In other words, a Wiccan practitioner can do anything, including spell casting, as long as nobody is harmed physically or mentally by their actions.

Widdershins: Movement in a counter-clockwise direction, to the left. The word derives from two Old German words meaning 'backward travel,' or 'going against.' It's considered unlucky, as, in medieval writings, demons apparently approached the Devil 'widdershins.' In Wicca, widdershins is used to close off the sacred circle when a ritual is finished, so the remaining energies can be returned to the Earth to be transmuted. Widdershins can also be used to offset harmful or bad magick.

Witch: A person, male or female, who practices magick.

Witchcraft: A pagan religion, working with the Earth and Nature to benefit people and the planet.

Yule: The sabbat celebrated on 21 December to celebrate the rebirth of the Horned God.

Further Reading and Online Resources on Wicca

Wicca is all about learning and growing spiritually through constant practice, study, and research. This book has merely scratched the surface of the theory and practice of Wicca, but there are many resources available online and in print to help you on your spiritual journey. Below are listed just some of the many reputable and useful websites and books which may help you along your Wiccan path. Blessed Be!

Wicca for Beginners by Thea Sabin

Wicca: A Guide for the Solitary Practitioner by Scott Cunningham

Living Wicca: A Further Guide for the Solitary Practitioner by Scott Cunningham

Wicca for Beginners: A Guide to Wiccan Beliefs, Rituals, Magic and Witchcraft by Lisa Chamberlain

Everyday Magic: Spells and Rituals for Modern Living by Dorothy Morrison

Wicca for One: The Path of Solitary Witchcraft by Raymond Buckland

Wiccan Roots: Gerald Gardner and the Modern Witchcraft Revival by Philip Heselton

The Wicca Spell Book by Gerina Dunwich

Wicca Candle Magic by Leonie Sage

Wicca: A Modern Guide to Witchcraft and Magick by Harmony Nice

Drawing Down the Moon by Margot Adler

There are literally thousands of books on Wicca and witchcraft out there, but this small selection is designed to help you progress on your journey in an interesting and entertaining manner.

Reputable Wiccan Websites

There is a vast amount of online resources about Wicca, but a little discrimination will come in handy here. Check that the site owner knows their stuff and is an experienced Wiccan practitioner who is qualified to teach others either through formal study or extended practice. Generally, those who have authored a number of books on the subject, such as Scott Cunningham, Lisa Chamberlain, and Raymond

Buckland can be trusted to offer good advice or to recommend reputable online resources. I have found these sites particularly useful over the last few years.

https://wicca.com/ This site – also known as The Celtic Connection – is one of the oldest, if not the oldest online resources for Wicca. It's been in existence since 1997. Lots of interesting, informative articles, and an excellent list of curated links to external sites.

http://blessedbe.sugarbane.com/ This is another informative, well-established site, and a very good resource for those new to the craft, with a lot to learn about all aspects of Wicca.

https://wiccanspells.info/ An excellent source of free Wiccan spells with lots of helpful information, as well as spells. Attractive layout, and an online shop for supplies. Online since 2012, it has grown from a small personal blog to an internationally respected authority on Wicca.

http://wiccaliving.com/ This website is hosted by best-selling author and eclectic solitary practitioner Lisa Chamberlain. Much of her material is written with beginning Wiccans in mind and is very accessible. Prepare to be on this site for hours!

https://www.wicca-spirituality.com/ Hosted by Erin Dragonsong, a Wiccan witch with 35 years experience, this is a fabulous free resource, where you can learn absolutely everything about Wicca. Over 300 articles, as well as the Wicca online 'school.'

https://www.free-witchcraft-spells.com/ Not just about spells, this site has a great section on beginning in Wicca, as well as lots of information to help you hone your skills, and details of courses on Wicca across the Internet. The webmaster has been a practicing witch for over 20 years.

This is just a small sample of some of the online resources I have used myself – there are much more available, but I've kept it brief, as it can all get a bit overwhelming. I hope you find this round-up of further reading and online resources helpful in your Wiccan journey. Blessed Be!

Made in the USA
Coppell, TX
03 January 2020

14035478R00104